Franciscan Nonviolence

Stories, Reflections, Principles, Practices, and Resources

Ken Butigan, Mary Litell, O.S.F., and Louis Vitale, O.F.M.

Pace e Bene Nonviolence Service

Sponsored by The OFM Justice, Peace and Integrity of Creation International Council and The Interfranciscan JPIC Commission

For information, please contact: Pace e Bene Nonviolence Service,
1420 W. Bartlett Ave., Las Vegas, NV 89106, USA. (702) 648-2281,
www.paceebene.org.

*Sponsored by The OFM Justice, Peace and Integrity of Creation
International Council and the Interfranciscan JPIC Commission*

Grateful acknowledgement is made to the following for permission to reprint
excerpts from copyrighted material from *Anthonian Magazine* written by Herman
Schaluck, O.F.M. © 1995 by St. Anthony's Guild. Reprinted by permission.
Excerpts from *Clare of Assisi: Early Documents* by Regis J. Armstrong, O.F.M.
Cap., copyright © 1988 by Paulist Press and reprinted by permission. Excerpts
from *Francis of Assisi: Early Documents, Vol. I, The Saint* edited by Regis
Armstrong, O.F.M. Cap., J. A. Wayne Hellman, O.F.M. Conv., and William Short,
O.F.M., copyright © 1999 by New City Press. Reprinted by permission. Excerpts
from *Francis of Assisi: Early Documents, Vol. II, The Founder* edited by Regis
Armstrong, O.F.M. Cap., J. A. Wayne Hellman, O.F.M. Conv., and William Short,
O.F.M., copyright © 2000 by New City Press. Reprinted by permission. Excerpts
from *Francis of Assisi: Early Documents, Vol. III, The Prophet* edited by Regis
Armstrong, O.F.M. Cap., J. A. Wayne Hellman, O.F.M. Conv., and William Short,
O.F.M., copyright © 2001 by New City Press. Reprinted by permission. Excerpts
from *From Violence To Wholeness: The Spirituality and Practice of Active
Nonviolence by* Ken Butigan with Patricia Bruno, O.P., copyright © 1999, 2002 by
Pace e Bene Nonviolence Service. Reprinted by permission.
Library of Congress Cataloging-in-Publication Data

ISBN: 0-9669783-9-0

**Franciscan nonviolence:
stories, reflections, principles, practices and resources**

Pace e Bene Nonviolence Service.
Design, Formatting and illustration

con
formando
conforma@prodigy.net.mx

Acknowledgements

We wish to express deep appreciation to the following individuals and organizations for their contributions to this publication: Francisco O'Conaire, O.F.M. of the OFM Justice, Peace and Integrity of Creation International Council and the Interfranciscan JPIC Commission, Sr. Celine, Joseph Chinnici, O.F.M. for conversations with Louis Vitale in March 2002 that provided invaluable insights on St. Francis's conversion, Ed Dunn, O.F.M., Rose Fernando, O.S.F., Rosemary Lynch, O.S.F., Fr. Pat McCloskey, O.F.M., Cynthia Okayama Dopke at Resources Advancing Initiatives for Nonviolence (RAIN) for editorial assistance, Ali Packard, Alain Richard, O.F.M., and Mark Schroeder, O.F.M.

Contents

Foreword   **7**

Introduction: Franciscan Roots of Active and
Transformative Nonviolence   **11**

Part 1. The Stories of St. Francis and St. Clare   **25**
of Assisi: Reflections on Active Nonviolence

Chapter 1. St. Francis's Conversion: *From Violence*   **26**
           to Wholeness

Chapter 2. St. Clare and a Community Without
           Distinctions of Class or Wealth: *Diversity*
           and Inclusion   **39**

Chapter 3. Nonviolent Intervention and Mediation:
           St. Francis and the Wolf of Gubbio   **45**

Chapter 4. Pluralism, Fundamentalism, and Active
           Nonviolence: *St. Francis's Meeting with*
           the Sultan   **52**

Chapter 5. Active Nonviolence and Restorative Justice:
           The Three Robbers at Monte Casale   **58**

Chapter 6. St. Clare and Relentless Persistence   **64**

Chapter 7. Processes of Reconciliation: *The Bishop*
           and the Mayor   **69**

Part 2. Resources for Active and Transformative Nonviolence   79

Decalogue for a Spirituality of Franciscan Nonviolence   80

Martin Luther King Jr.'s Principles of Nonviolence   82

Putting Active Nonviolence Into Practice: *A Four-Step Process of Conflict Resolution*   84

Daily Practices to Cultivate Franciscan Nonviolence   87

The Relationship Between Trauma and the Practice of Active and Transformative Nonviolence   92

A Sample Agenda for a Two-Hour Session on Violence and Transformative Nonviolence   95

Lessons From Experience - Becoming Peacemakers: *Reflections on Negotiating Peace*   102

Franciscan Publications on Nonviolence   112

Select List of Nonviolence Organizations and Internet Resources   115

Select Bibliography on Nonviolence   119

FOREWORD

This little book has been produced by Pace e Bene Nonviolence Service at the request of the Animation Committee of the OFM Justice, Peace, and Integrity of Creation International Council and with the endorsement of the Interfranciscan JPIC Commission (IFCJP).

As Franciscans we are deeply disturbed by the violence in the world and our increasingly deadly potential to destroy life on this planet. The roots of violence are within each of us, as are the solutions to overcome it and build a more just and peaceful world. We are appalled by the wanton and dramatic violence that takes innocent lives, as in the case of what occurred on September 11, 2001 in the United States. We are also profoundly disturbed by the hundreds of thousands of our brothers and sisters, particularly in the Two-Thirds world, who are being silently killed by the political and economic policies of the privileged, by people more concerned to preserve their self-interest than to create a sustainable world for all it's creatures.

As Franciscans we need to reclaim our role as peacemakers. We have a strong tradition full of inspirational men and women of peace and reconciliation, inspired by the particular way both St. Francis and

7

St. Clare lived the gospel's call to build just relationships based on respect, equality and the search for harmony. Unless there are more people willing to use their intelligence and creativity to pursue peace tenaciously, many soldiers are willing to train, fight and die by the use of arms to achieve their objectives, continuing the vicious cycle of violence and counter violence. Franciscan Peacemakers are not pacifists, if we mean by that term those who are "passive" or who simply "pacify" without working for justice. To be true to our vocation we must be proactive in confronting the causes of violence as well as their manifestations. We need to desire this with all our hearts. The challenge is to recognize and overcome the violence in ourselves as well as to learn strategies to deal with numerous actual and emerging conflict in our societies. Just as there are people willing to die by the sword, the world needs people who have overcome the fear of death, committed to nonviolent means of transforming and resolving differences and conflicts.

This book is intended to briefly show that nonviolence is a gospel as well as a Franciscan value. Nonviolence has not failed, it has yet to be tried in its fullest sense. Those who have committed their lives to peaceful and nonviolent resolution of conflict can teach us much, if we are willing to listen and learn. This book intends to inspire and point in this direction. For those who wish to pursue this road and learn, more resources are available.

Originally this book was intended for reflection at the local level by the Franciscan community. Due to the extensive nature of the volume, we additionally recommend its use for initial and ongoing formation programs, seminars and retreats. It could be incorporated into existing programs by including nonviolence as an integral dimension to our lives and ministry.

We wish to thank Pace e Bene Nonviolence Service for offering this valuable and inspirational resource for the continuing formation of Franciscans as well as those who translated it into several languages. We thank the many brothers and sisters who are living and promoting active nonviolence.

OFM JPIC Rome Office and IFCJP Commission

*...This is the peace
proclaimed and given to us
by our Lord Jesus Christ
and preached again and again
by our father Francis.*

*At the beginning and end of every
sermon he announced peace;
in every greeting he wished for
peace;
in every contemplation he sighed for
ecstatic peace....*

St. Bonaventure,
The Journey of the Mind to God[1]

INTRODUCTION

Franciscan Roots of Transformative Nonviolence

Where there is charity and wisdom,
there is neither fear nor ignorance.
Where there is patience and humility,
there is neither anger nor disturbance.
Where there is poverty with joy,
there is neither greed nor avarice.
Where there is rest and meditation,
there is neither anxiety nor restlessness.
Where there is fear of the Lord to guard an entrance,
there the enemy cannot have a place to enter.
Where there is a heart full of mercy and discernment,
there is neither excess nor hardness of heart.

Francis of Assisi[2]

What difference would it make if we really believed that God is a God of creative, abundant and thoroughgoing nonviolence? If we truly believed this, how would it change our lives and the life of the world?

What difference would it make if we really believed that God longs for us to nurture what Martin Luther King, Jr. named the Beloved Community, where *all* sit down together at the Great Banquet and revel in one another's differences without recourse to violence? What

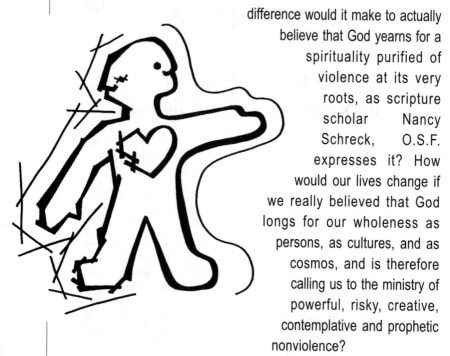

difference would it make to actually believe that God yearns for a spirituality purified of violence at its very roots, as scripture scholar Nancy Schreck, O.S.F. expresses it? How would our lives change if we really believed that God longs for our wholeness as persons, as cultures, and as cosmos, and is therefore calling us to the ministry of powerful, risky, creative, contemplative and prophetic nonviolence?

We live in a world of great external violence – physical, emotional, psychological, institutional, and structural – as well as within our own beings. This book is offered as a way of acknowledging the deeply rooted patterns of violence within and without and to meditate on the possibilities of active nonviolence in such a world.

Specifically, we reflect in this volume on the dynamics and creative power of Franciscan nonviolence. This Franciscan tradition offers us ways to reflect on the God of nonviolent love and how this nonviolent God is calling us to cultivate the spirituality and practice of active nonviolence in our lives and in the larger life of the world.

Today's Spiritual Challenge and Opportunity

In every age we are invited to become our truest selves in very specific and challenging ways. In our own era of rapid globalization, this deeply spiritual challenge involves facing the many obstacles that threaten our wholeness at every level. Economic exploitation, cultural destruction, racism, sexism, homophobia and ecological devastation are systemic forms of violence and injustice that endanger both our survival and this profound hunger for wholeness and integrity. Violence is any verbal, emotional, physical, institutional or social-structural behavior or condition that dominates, dehumanizes, diminishes or destroys ourselves or others.

The pervasive structures of violence we face today are rooted, in turn, in deeply embedded impulses of fear, hate and greed. These impulses often nurture separation and instill a seemingly unbridgeable gap between "us" and "them." We often project our own violence onto one another; we repeatedly see those with whom we struggle as unambiguously evil; we customarily justify cultural and economic systems that devalue other beings; and we often deploy the implements of verbal, emotional or physical war to both protect ourselves and to create what we think is justice. "The myth of redemptive violence," as scripture scholar Walter Wink names it, pervades our consciousness and our cultures.

Our greatest contemporary spiritual crisis is one of faith. The temptation is to place our faith in the power of violence rather than the force of the good; to surrender to violence forgetting that humanity, while capable of both love and violence, is created in the image, the very likeness of a good God. Our greatest challenge today is to cultivate a path as individuals and communities throughout the world that actively

13

proclaims this goodness. In this way we might challenge the patterns of violence, and open ourselves to the transforming grace of the Nonviolent God.

Francis, Clare, and Faith-Based Nonviolence

Although the word "nonviolence" was not coined until 1923, the dynamic of nonviolence understood as a creative and integrative power is, as Mohandas Gandhi put it, "as old as the hills." Francis and Clare of Assisi envisioned, cultivated and experimented with this nonviolent power in their own lives and in the transforming Franciscan movement they founded. In the Prologue to his *Itinerarium,* St. Bonaventure uses the word "peace" ten times. He uses it to describe God's presence and power, referring to God's minister of peace, St. Francis. Clearly, the ministry of peace figured significantly in the path Francis walked. In this book we reflect on this peace, how it came to play such an important role in Francis's spirituality and how we can promote this ministry today.

Francis of Assisi, the son of a wealthy merchant, grew up steeped in the vision of chivalric honor and romantic love. After a somewhat reckless youth, he saw combat in a war between Assisi and a neighboring city-state. During one of the battles he was captured and spent a year as a prisoner of war. After being ransomed by his father, Francis underwent a profound conversion experience, prompted by an encounter with a leper where he overcame a reaction of physical aversion and was able to see him as Christ in his midst.

Francis experienced a full transformation of identity in 1208 when he took radically to heart the thoroughgoing demand of Matthew 19:21, Jesus' call to the rich young man to give everything away and follow him. Francis, burning with the desire to imitate the poor and crucified Jesus, renounced all claims to his family's wealth and espoused "Lady Poverty" or "Holy Poverty" as his lifelong companion.

In 1212 he was joined in his work by Clare of Assisi. Francis was born into a family that represented one center of power of Assisi life, the emerging mercantile class, while Clare was born into a clan that represented the other, the long-established nobility. In tandem, their renunciation of the typical life of the times served as a complementary and virtually complete rejection of the world of getting, spending and dominating.

Francis's vow of voluntary poverty was an intuitive critique of the growing economic and social disparities in thirteenth-century Europe as it witnessed the shift from rural to urban life, the rise of the merchant class, the coming end to feudalism and emerging monarchies as well as nation-states. These historical factors were creating an increasingly stratified society that led to involuntary poverty.

Francis was convinced that God was the "Most High" who was Transcendent Goodness, a goodness lavished freely, everywhere. To become voluntarily poor was to share the plight of the poor but also to share in the life of God, who gives everything. This Trinitarian God – known in the magnificence of life, in the crucified Jesus and in the Holy Spirit who is actively vivifying all that exists – was, for Francis, worthy of praise and endless gratitude. It was with these convictions that Francis finally became a "troubadour" – not as a singer of earthly honor and romantic love but as a singer of the God who loves us with infinite mercy and tenderness.

Franciscans "Serving Peace"

However imperfectly realized over the succeeding eight centuries, the ministry of peacemaking – recognizing the primordial presence of God's peace deep within and serving it with prayer and action– has persisted as a central dimension of Franciscan spirituality. As we see in the stories featured in this text, Francis vigorously counseled peace between warring city-states and between Christians and Muslims. His devotion to embodied peacemaking and nonviolent intervention is captured paradigmatically in the story of the Wolf of Gubbio where Francis brokered a resolution between an Italian village and a wolf by meeting the needs of both sides. This is even more compellingly demonstrated in visit with Malik-al-Kamil, the sultan of Egypt. During the fifth crusade in 1219, "in the midst of wartime, Francis went to the enemy *unarmed* and *loved the enemy as a brother.*" Francis attempted to embody Jesus' words to "love the enemy" and to face the enemy within.[3]

St. Francis and St. Clare of Assisi greeted the people of their time with the expression "Pace e bene!" or "Peace and good!" So much was expressed by this little phrase: *May you have the fullness of well-being, may you be secure and happy; may you not want; may your dignity be respected; may the goodness in your inmost being flourish; may the world in which we live know this deep peace.* It was a blessing, a hope, and a way of acknowledging the sacredness of those whom they encountered.

The first Rule of the Third Order admonishes the brothers and sisters that they are "not to bear arms for any reason." The Franciscan movement became so widespread that there are indications that, in parts of medieval Europe, war was stymied at various times during the Middle Ages because potential soldiers had become Franciscans and were bound by their vows not to engage in armed conflict.

Even a cursory glance at the writings of Francis that have come down to us reveals his concern with the spirit and practice of nonviolence as he urges his brothers to follow Jesus' call to love their enemies, and do good to those who would seem to be their enemies; to go among people as Jesus instructed his disciples, in simplicity, as peacemakers, and calling nothing their own but sharing with everyone.

Francis lived, as we do, in an era marked by violence. His defeat, imprisonment and illness at Perugia suggest that he suffered from we now call Post-Traumatic Stress Disorder. In the wake of this profound encounter with violence and the crisis it provoked, Francis became a person of peace who greeted all with "Pace e bene" ("Peace and goodness!"). Francis's peacemaking was rooted in three gospel-based convictions:

1. God is all good, and all good comes from God

Francis experienced God as the source of all good, the God of unconditional love. Creative, abundant and thoroughgoing nonviolence is another way of describing this unconditional love. Francis sought to live in such a way that this divine goodness and compassion were transparently present in himself, in others, and in all of creation. This divine goodness and compassion is the source of true peace.

2. The gospel way is a way of active love

To love our enemies, to turn the other cheek, to feed the hungry, to lay down one's life –these, Francis indicates, are not forms of passivity and resignation but active affirmations and instances of Jesus' Reign of God. While warning that "all who take up the sword will perish by the sword" (Matt. 26:52), Jesus rebukes the disciples who request permission to call down fire from heaven on inhospitable Samaritans (Luke 9:51-56). That war-like activity is familiar to us listening to accounts of bombing strikes in contemporary warfare on nearly every continent. Jesus urges a transformation based on compassion, bearing one another's burdens, loving one's enemies, sharing one's goods with each other. In the end, he asks for forgiveness for those who put him to death for "they do not know what they are doing" (Luke 34: 24).

3. Voluntary poverty serves and sustains true peace

Wealth is often rooted in the injustice of exploitation of humanity and the earth. At the same time, when wealth is accumulated, there is the problem of its defense. In short, wealth is created out of inequality and because of inequality it provokes a defensive posture, a willingness to go to war to defend one's wealth. If we don't have anything, there is nothing to defend. Or if we do have things, they are to be shared, not hoarded. Archaeological evidence has emerged from the Middle East that when houses were basically of the same size, peace prevailed. When there began to be a disparity in the size of people's houses, more evidence of social conflict and war emerges. The way of nonviolence is not only a way of responding to specific forms of violence. Rather, nonviolence is a holistic way of life that is truly a spiritual pursuit that effects the way we respond to God, to our neighbor, to ourselves, and to all of creation.

Franciscan Peacemaking Today

Friar Alain Richard, O.F.M., a longtime practitioner of active nonviolence, suggests that "there are deep connections between the nonviolence of the Gandhian nonviolent methods, imbued with the gospel of the Beatitudes and the example of Christ, and the Franciscan way of taking the gospel seriously."[4] Alain finds a Franciscan affinity with fundamental elements of nonviolence in that they are based on a deep compassion which recognizes that all people –our adversaries as much as ourselves– are capable of both good and evil. This is a compassionate love that is respectful of all, including all of creation. It leads to a deep solidarity to which we are called today, toward all the living, enabling us to share their suffering. Friar Alain notes that the strongest locus of nonviolence today is among the poor in their struggles for survival, and that we who have chosen voluntary poverty often find ourselves in their midst.

This sense of things has been dramatically evident over the past several decades. In the 1980s, for example, many nonviolent movements for freedom emerged throughout the world, mostly among the disinherited of the earth, changing the political landscape in the Philippines, South Africa, parts of Eastern Europe and Latin America. Franciscans worldwide found themselves taking part in, supporting and being affected by this process of nonviolent transformation. That spreading interest in nonviolence throughout the Franciscan world has flowered since then in local, national and international projects at the service of creative nonviolence.

Many people question nonviolence because they interpret it as passivity in the face of violence and destruction. But Jesus was not passive. He engaged, even resisted, those who were violent and oppressive. A contemporary strand of biblical scholarship, notably articulated by scripture scholar Walter Wink, describes this as Jesus' "third way" of active love –a way that is neither passive nor violent. Wink's scriptural interpretation, for example, suggests that Jesus' admonition "do not resist an evildoer" means "do not resist *violently*."[5] Wink interprets Jesus' call to "turn the other cheek," "strip off one's clothing," and "carry the pack the extra mile," as creative and powerful responses to injustice that expose the violence of the oppressors, create dilemmas for the oppressor, and compel the oppressor to see the humanity of those whom he or she is violating.[6] Jesus calls us to engage the opponent in a way that challenges unjust attitudes and structures while creating the opportunity for both parties to be saved from the demonic cycle of oppression.

These fundamental evangelical principles have been substantiated in our own day by nonviolence practitioners. Martin Luther King, Jr., toward the end of his life, stated that the stark choice before humanity was now "nonviolence or nonexistence." The way of violence will stimulate a cycle of retaliatory violence that, given the grimly awesome terror humanity is now capable of wreaking, can spin unimaginably out of control. Jesus' "third way" is seen by King as increasingly our most realistic option.

In our day, as in Francis's day, the Spirit urges us to experiment with nonviolence. In surprising ways, we –like Francis and his companions– find ourselves influenced by and participating in movements impelled by hunger for spiritual renewal, for justice and peace, for compassion and reverence for all creation. While there are figures of heroic stature like Mohandas Gandhi, Martin Luther King, Jr. and Aung San Suu Kyi who have demonstrated the power of nonviolence, the transformation of our world today through compassionate, active nonviolence, is being carried out by masses of people on every continent whose situations call forth from them courage, compassion and creativity.

Drawing on the vision and practice of Jesus, Clare and Francis, Gandhi and many others, these projects have been experimenting with creative and transformative nonviolence understood as *an ongoing process of personal and social transformation that is a way off being and acting rooted in the power of love, in the desire for the well-being of all, and in the longing to end the cycle of personal, interpersonal, and social-structural violence.* This transformative nonviolence often includes:

- Making contact with the woundedness and sacredness in our lives and the lives of others;
- Creatively and courageously opening safe space for active listening and for acknowledging that each of us has a piece of the truth;
- Transforming Us vs. Them thinking and doing;
- Seeking to recognize and actively transform coercive and dominative differences of power;

- Mobilizing nonviolent person-power and people-power as creative alternatives to patterns of domination, to passive acceptance of those patterns, or to counter-violence as a way of challenging those patterns; and
- Taking initiatives to change the dynamics of violence by creating just and compassionate solutions that genuinely address the causes of conflict.

The way of active nonviolence is drawing us into a renewed and ongoing spiritual formation process. In this process we are learning to compassionately challenge our own patterns; to de-center and re-center the self that has been shaped by patterns of violence in our families, in our churches, in our societies. We find ourselves taking action that helps us "act our way" into new thinking, feeling, and believing. Indeed, we are discovering how the source and meaning of our lives –our God who has given us life and sustains us– is a Nonviolent God who longs for this wholeness for us and for all beings, a God who calls us to experiment with and embody this "nonviolent life" in the healing of ourselves, our families, our communities, and our world.

This Book

This book is an effort to reflect on the path of Franciscan peacemaking by members of one of the emerging Franciscan projects, Pace e Bene, which began in Las Vegas, Nevada USA in 1989. While there are many other resources on nonviolence (some of which we note in the bibliography at the end), we hope this modest work will move us forward on the way of peace through nonviolence that Francis and Clare walked in their times.

Many of the stories about Francis and Clare that have come down to us reflect their teaching and practice of nonviolence. In this volume we reflect on seven of these stories as a way of illuminating a variety of approaches to peacemaking that are embedded in the earliest experiences of our tradition. These accounts suggest important aspects of the journey of active nonviolence, including conversion to peacemaking, nonviolent intervention and mediation, negotiating difference in a respectful and compassionate way, restorative justice and reconciliation. Finally, we offer contemporary examples of ordinary people, some of them Franciscans, participating in the movements and events of our times. In their lives and in these movements we can see examples of the dynamics and power of transformative nonviolence.

In each of the following seven sections, we present a story, drawing on early Franciscan sources, that highlights a particular approach to putting active nonviolence into practice. This is followed by a commentary on this story that draws out its themes and dynamics of nonviolence. Finally, we offer contemporary Franciscan and non-Franciscan examples of these dynamics in action. This is then followed by a section on principles of active nonviolence and guidelines for mediating conflict, a sample agenda for communal reflection on nonviolence, and resources for further exploration.

PART 1

The Stories of St. Francis and St. Clare of Assisi:

Reflections on Active Nonviolence

1 St. Francis's Conversion: From Violence to Wholeness

Once there was a great massacre in a war between the citizens of Perugia and Assisi. Francis was captured along with many others, and chained with the rest of them, endured the squalor of prison.[7]

[After a long recuperation from his imprisonment, Francis tried again to be a heroic warrior and to join a crusade.]

When [Francis] set out for Apulia, he got as far as Spoleto, where he began to feel a little ill. No less anxious about the trip, as he was falling asleep, half awake, he heard someone asking him where he wanted to go. When Francis revealed to him his entire plan, the other said: "Who can do more good for you, the Lord or the servant?" When [Francis] answered him: "The Lord," he said to him: "Then why are you abandoning the Lord for the servant, the patron for the client?" And Francis said: "Lord what do you want me to do?" "Go back to your land," he said, "and what you are to do will be told to you. You must understand in another way the vision which you saw."[8]

Francis of Assisi: Early Documents

Reflection

Nonviolence often arises in the context of violence. In his book, *Francis of Assisi*, Arnaldo Fortini illustrates the barbarity of the era in which Francis lived. He quotes warriors of that time: "It is good to see war tents spread out in the meadows, to hear the cry of an attack, to look at the dead lying in trenches, pierced by the stumps of bannered lances."[9] No torture seemed too great as the perpetrators and bystanders gloried in the blood and gore. They rejoiced in battle and body count, which Fortini insists they saw as giving joy to life. It also gave power and riches.

At the time of Francis, civil war existed in Assisi between the rich and poor, the haves and the have-nots. These were wars fought for power and economic gain. The new merchants fought the nobility. A very bloody war between Assisi and Perugia broke out in 1202. A 20-year-old Francis marched off in a spirit of exhilaration and glory. But the Assisians were overrun and beaten. Fortini writes that the "sight of those killed on the field where the fighting took place was horrifying beyond words...all [the fields] were covered with the dead. 'How disfigured are the bodies on the field of battle, and how mutilated and broken the members.'...Assisi was appalled by the massacre... A great many of Assisi were taken prisoner.... Among them was Francis.... That battle with all its raw ferocity and bloodthirsty pride, the sight of the dead, and the infinite grief made in Francis's warm and generous spirit a wound so deep that time never healed it. ...Anyone who lives through the soul-searing instant of madness when meeting an enemy knows the nightmare that comes later."[10]

After the battle of Collestrada, Francis was taken to Perugia and imprisoned. He was one of the fortunate ones. The archers and infantrymen were butchered, but the knights and those riding horses were held for ransom. Francis's prison was miserable, crowded and brutal. Francis made efforts to overcome the brutality and lift the spirits of his fellow-prisoners. Nevertheless, he succumbed to severe illness. This ultimately enabled his father to ransom him. Francis had to suffer through a long convalescence, attended to by his loving mother. He did recover his health. But Celano notes: "From that day he began to regard himself as worthless and to hold in contempt what he had previously held as admirable and lovable."[11]

Francis had not completely lost the hunger for battle and the longing for glory that was so much a part of his culture. Once again he set out to join a great knight, Walter of Brienne, in a campaign with the papal militia. He was even enticed into this crusade by a dream of his house filled with arms, shields and other implements of war. He saw this as a sign of success as he set out for Apulia and battle and glory. But a voice spoke to him and asked, "Who can do more good for you, the Lord or the servant?" and then urged him to go back to his own land where he would be told what to do. Francis returned to Assisi, resumed some of his prodigal ways, but then encountered a leper, whom he kissed, and heard a voice from the cross calling him to rebuild the church.

Thus a very radical transformation began. Francis's eagerness to provide for the poor, and his desire to be in the company of lepers and the outcast move him to an entirely different class in life. This was most dramatically illustrated when he went before the Bishop Guido and offered all his means, and even all his clothes, to his father.

Francis took the words of the cross seriously and began to literally repair churches; he also joined in a very caring way with the poor and the lepers. Francis had made a dramatic social change. He had

alienated himself from his family and his social grouping. In our contemporary usage, Francis had made a radical, preferential option for the poor.

Francis and Nonviolence

The focus in this volume is not just on Francis's conversion from a life of pleasure, frivolity and excess to a devout follower of Christ. We are especially interested in the way that Francis follows, in particular, the *nonviolence* of Christ.

Nonviolence emerges, as noted above, in the midst of violence. The more dramatic the violence, the stronger the temptation to respond in turn with violence. But horrific violence also stimulates the opposite in some people. Some people, rather than desiring to retaliate, seek instead an alternative. They are

29

motivated to experiment with active nonviolence. How might this have been true in the life of St. Francis?

Fortini describes the horrors of war and the impact this warfare had on Francis. Francis likely shed blood in the Perugia campaign. In the wake of this war and its brutality, Francis conceivably suffered from what today is described as Post-Traumatic Stress Disorder (PTSD). This term, though popularized during the Vietnam War, applies to veterans of all wars and to survivors of other very traumatic events. While sufferers of Post-Traumatic Stress Disorder sometime seek out new forms of violence and conflict, in many cases they seek to avoid conflict. They also demonstrate diminished interest or participation in activities they previously enjoyed; often they feel detached from others and withdraw from the external world, frequently experiencing recurring nightmares, sleeplessness, depression, hopelessness, irritation and anger. Francis experienced the trauma of war and bore many of the marks of a survivor of war. Dealing with anger was a continual challenge. In his later years he suffered from depression. He experienced sleeplessness, nightmares and dramatic dreams; he even lost interest in things he had previously enjoyed, including spending time in nature.

Common to many people who endure war or imprisonment is "survivor's guilt." It is not improbable that Francis's exceptional concern for the poor was rooted, in part, in an abiding awareness that the poor Assisians who fought with him in the war against Perugia had been slaughtered while he, the son of a rich merchant, had instead been held for ransom. An acute consciousness of this burden –the burden of being given back his life while others had not– may have played a role in his abandoning the privilege that had spared his life. This awareness may have provoked a dramatic reversal of his desire for riches which yielded its opposite: the longing to marry Lady Poverty and to live the fate of the poor himself. All of these are the qualities that made Francis a saint, a sanctity that may have been spawned in a conscious struggle with the brutality of war and its cloying aftermath.

Many who suffer from post-traumatic stress continue a life of violence under many guises. Some end their lives in prison or meet a violent death. Some recover, some do not. The severity of the trauma is often a predictor. For Francis the conditions were, as Fortini suggests, extremely severe. But Francis had the unique grace to turn these disorders into a path toward holiness.

One of the most important ways to treat great stress is meditation. Francis entered caves in the hills and drew very close to God. He re-engaged with nature. He gave himself in service to others, often a remarkably curative activity. He sought to re-write the "script," as when he went before the Sultan with only a cross. He overcame his fear of robbers and wolves. He treated all –especially those with leprosy– with deep respect, cherishing each one as bearing the face of Christ. In these and many other ways he overcame the violence within himself and healed the trauma. His close relationships with the Brothers and with Clare brought him into a new and profound sense of community. These are traits of the way of nonviolence, including the principles of nonviolence enumerated in this study. They call for a deep transformation of heart as we seek to live out what Martin Luther King, Jr. refers to as the "Beloved Community." Francis's deep appreciation of every person led him to see no one as enemy. He preferred to welcome enemies into his midst.

Although Francis started out as a combatant, he became a conscientious objector. He withdrew from his commitment to the Crusade of Walter of Brienne and embodied a commitment of

31

disarmament by carrying a cross, not a sword, when approaching the Sultan.

Moreover, he encouraged others not to take up the sword. As Former Minister General of the Friars Minor, Herman Schaluck noted, "He forbade all of his followers to carry weapons. As a result, it became difficult for some feudal lords to muster an army together, as there were so many Secular Franciscans who refused to carry arms. This simple demand by Francis helped to collapse the feudal system in Europe."[12] As Brother Herman writes, Francis is an apt model in our own day, for he once saw war as a road to glory, but eventually came to see its human devastation. Such awareness is especially acutely needed today with carpet bombing, smart bombs, terrorism, and embargoes that strangle the lives of children. As Schaluck suggests, there are indications that Francis helped bring about the abolition of war in certain parts of Europe during some periods of the Middle Ages.

Ultimately, we are speaking of a deep religious conversion. Francis transcended the extreme violence of his times –with which he himself was originally fascinated and in which he eagerly participated– and was touched and transformed by the compassion of God. He recognized, perhaps while in battle or in prison, that there is a woundedness *and* a sacredness in every person and in all of creation.

This is the starting point of nonviolence. The transforming power of nonviolence begins and ends with an awareness of the presence of God. It is this presence that breaks the spiral of violence. The Spirit of our unifying God is present when conflict is resolved, when the script of violence is rewritten to embrace the sacredness of all parties and when creativity is used to break the cycle of retaliation. Moving from his woundedness, through his dramatic illness, Francis achieves a deep conversion that overcame the dominant drive for violence. He came to see that an all-loving God is a God of compassion. Human beings are meant to love and be loved, radically and totally. This dynamic challenges us to overcome the divisions that separate us and to discover the underlying sacredness that unites us.

Francis comes, finally, to understand his true vocation, the calling to love one another as God has loved us. In practical terms this means resisting the tendency of violence to divide the world into various enemy camps. Practitioners of nonviolence seek to become their truest selves by slowly learning to love all beings, especially their enemies. In verse 38 of his *Later Admonition and Exhortation to the Brothers and Sisters of Penance* Francis exhorts us "We must love our enemies and do good to those who hate us."[13]

In verse 23 of his *Testament,* Francis tells us that "The Lord revealed a greeting to me that we should say: 'May the Lord give you peace.'"[14] Bonaventure recalls, "At the beginning and end of every sermon he announced peace; in every greeting he wished for peace."[15] Francis instructs his brothers, as they enter someone's house, to say "Peace to this house."

Historian and theologian Joseph Chinnici, O.F.M. asks the question: "Why does Francis use these greetings which, historically speaking, were unusual and uncommon at that time?" Chinnici suggests that these greetings of peace comprise a social act. They are a call to overcome the dominant violence of the times and the system of dominance that fosters and promotes violence. To seek such peace is a communal action; it is active nonviolence. It addresses the structure of violence, as well as the political and economic systems that separate peoples into warring parties. Chinnici asserts that the central thrust of Francis's life pursuit was to overcome violence with a new call for peace.

Chinnici suggests Francis's underlying Christology: addressing and seeking to transform violence leads us to be more like Christ. Francis, through his own experience of violence, identified with the one who overcame violence. Francis identified with the one who told Peter to put down the sword and who healed the servant's ear. Francis identified with the one who, on the cross, prayed, "Father forgive them for they know not what they do." Francis's stigmata was an identification with this nonviolent Christ from deep within, a sign of his full conversion from a man of war to a man of peace.

The greeting of Christ after his resurrection was "Peace be with you." Francis bore that message to the world of his time. Chinnici notes that Francis sums up his life project of professing peace with the *Canticle of All Creation*, which Chinnici calls "A Cosmic Hymn of Peace." All creatures are identified as brothers and sisters. All participate in God, who created everything. So it is inevitable to practice peace. This remains a challenge for our times. To do this, Chinnici suggests, we "need armies of brothers and sisters who manifest peace."

CONTEMPORARY EXPERIENCES
Steps for Peace in South Asia

Br. Philip Hira O.F.M., Director NCJP Hyderabad, Pakistan.

Greetings from Hyderabad, Pakistan. I would like to share with you what the National Commission for Justice and Peace along with the Justice and Peace Commission and other nongovernmental organizations (NGOs) are trying to achieve here in Pakistan for the promotion of peace in our region.

I returned to Pakistan on 6th May, 2002 after attending the 58th United Nations Session on Human Rights in Geneva and Hyderabad Harrlem relationship programs in Holland. The whole country seemed involved in war preparations against India. Our television, radio, and newspapers were all projecting strong fear of war and worse, an atomic war between these two poor countries.

We at the office decided we must try to take steps to prevent the war. We contacted different NGOs and formulated our plan of action for prevention of war.

1. Awareness Program
We organized different community meetings with local political and social groups where we highlighted the aftereffects of war and especially atomic war. We shared what happened at Nagasaki and Hiroshima in Japan. We also showed distractions caused by wars within the subcontinent and whole world. We appealed to people that they should get actively involved to prevent this war and work for the promotion of peace.

2. Human Rights Activists Meeting
NCJP called a meeting of Human Rights activists from all over the Sindh to reflect on the country's situation and encourage them to organize peace awareness programs in their regions. We also requested them to meet the press people to ask that they write more for peace in their newspapers and magazines.

3. Peace Rally in Hyderabad
Different NGOs organized a peace march in Hyderabad on 27th May, 2002. Two hundred men and women belonging to different groups

came together in front of the Hyderabad Press Club. Local artists presented a drama highlighting Nagasaki's and Hiroshima's pains and demanded from leaders of Pakistan and India not to get engaged in useless war activity.

The procession marched through Hyderabad city with placards and banners projecting the need for peace and respect for nature and human life. On completion of our march a joint statement was read and distributed among press people. All people of good will belonging to different religious, ethnic and political groups are concerned and working together for promotion of Peace and Harmony.

Another War Veteran's Journey from Violence to Wholeness

Nearly 800 years after Francis experienced the horrors of war in Perugia, Dave experienced the horrors of war in Vietnam. Wounded, he began to die and was brought back from the edge of death. Since then, his life –like that of so many veterans– has been marked by his encounter with "Sister Death." While he does not consider himself a religious person, Dave realizes now that we are "made of something like small particles of light; we are connected to everyone and everything."

While Dave was working as a supervisor on the construction of a new church for a small Franciscan parish, he shared an experience with Sister Deborah, the Associate Pastor. He told her that he had no words to explain it and thought people would not understand or believe him. The description of his experience, however, was reminiscent of the question posed by Thomas Merton, the monk, mystic and nonviolence advocate: *How can you tell people that they are walking around radiant like stars?*

As Dave and Pastor Deborah's conversations continued, Dave went through a conversion to a new understanding of himself and our world, like that of Francis, that has changed his life. He is able to speak with others about a world in which we and all creatures are related, are shining with light. In his small world, his journey through violence to wholeness resembles that of Francis.

Dr. Yusuf Omar al-Azhari: Ambassador of Forgiveness

Dr. Yusuf Omar al-Azhari, former Somali Ambassador to the U.S. and his country's representative of Somalia to the United Nations, experienced six years of imprisonment following a military coup in his country. For the first six months of that time, he was held in solitary confinement and tortured daily. Fearful of going insane from hatred and desperation, he turned, finally, to prayer and experienced God's presence in his life. His journey to wholeness began in that prison. From that time on, he has been working to bring about peace and reconciliation in Somalia. He and several others who participated in a failed process to resolve the civil war and ensuing deadlock in Somali politics decided to work at the village level to break through the antagonism, mistrust and grievances from years of violence. As the work of reconciliation continues and a political reconstruction of the country slowly grows, they are convinced that forgiveness, with the grace of Allah, is the key factor in reaching the hearts of everyone. [16]

Reflection Question

What experiences in your own life, community and culture are examples of the challenges and possibilities of conversion to a life of gospel nonviolence?

2 St. Clare and A Community Without Distinctions of Class or Wealth: Diversity and Inclusion

If, by divine inspiration, anyone should come to us with the desire to embrace this life, the Abbess is required to seek the consent of all the sisters...[17] In the election of the Abbess the sisters are bound to observe the canonical form.[18] Likewise, if at any time it should appear to the entire body of the sisters that she [the Abbess] is not competent for their service and common welfare, the sisters are bound to elect another as Abbess and mother as soon as possible according to the form given above.[19]

39

She [the Abbess] should preserve the common life in everything, especially regarding all in the church, dormitory, refectory, infirmary, and in clothing...[20]

At least once a week the Abbess is required to call her sisters together in Chapter...[21] *There, too, she should consult with all her sisters on whatever concerns the welfare and good of the monastery; for the Lord often reveals what is best to the less [among us].*[22]

To preserve the unity of mutual love and peace, all who hold offices in the monastery should be chosen by the common consent of all the sisters.[23]

The Rule of Saint Clare

Reflection

When Clare of Assisi was beginning her way of life together with other women of Assisi and the surrounding area, she was given a rule to follow that was modeled on the rule for Cistercian women. This included the title of Abbess for the woman who would guide the community. While she was finally persuaded to accept this title, she disowned its accrued status thus she refused even the status of Abbess within a community committed to loving relationship without distinctions based in class, wealth or status. This is the basis to a nonviolent way of life and to the practice of active nonviolence. This radical departure for her time offers much for our consideration today.

In this community, embracing the poverty of Christ meant following Christ, who did not cling to the "status" of his divine nature, but rather embraced fully the human condition in all its beauty and in all its frailty. In such a community, the beauty and fragility of each person was to be embraced by all without distinction. The youngest, newest member of this community had the same right to speak in the weekly meetings as had every other sister.

Consensus was the way of decision-making. There were no servants, no special rooms or suites, no distinct classes of membership.

Neither Clare nor Francis used the terms "community" or "common life." What they did speak about was relationship, concretely: brothers and sisters. More than "common life," it was relatedness as sisters and brothers that they valued. And the way of life that each founder proposed supported and protected this relatedness. Clare referred to herself always in the context of her relationship with her sisters and brothers: as handmaid of the sisters; as a little plant of Francis; or, in letters, "...you make up most wonderfully what is lacking both in me and in the other sisters..." "...remember me and my sisters...."[24]

Clare could have remained within the walls of Assisi, within her own household and continued to lead the penitential life with family, friends and servants alike. In the end, she opted to move away from the city to live in a structure of inclusive, loving relationship with women from families of serfs, peasants, merchants and nobility, thus creating a new social structure for her times.

Much of the movement of active nonviolence today aims to create the social and economic structures that foster this same kind of inclusive, respectful relationship: diversity training; economic alternatives based in mutuality rather than exploitation; land reform that respects the earth and whole creation community, to name a few.

CONTEMPORARY EXPERIENCES
Multi-Racial Communities

For several years the Franciscan Missionaries of Mary in a Sri Lanka province have made a clear option to live in multi-racial communities as a Franciscan witness to racial harmony in the context of an ethnic war. A few years ago, the situation was very tense on the east coast, where there is a predominantly Tamil population. The Franciscan Missionaries of Mary had three Tamil-speaking sisters and one Sinhala-speaking sister in the community. At that point in our history, the Tamil militants had ordered that all the Sinhalese people leave that region. Those who had not

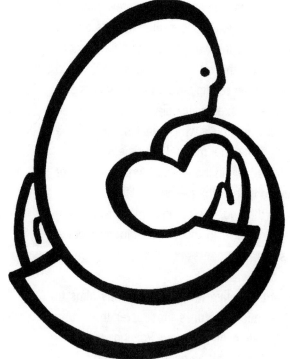

left, they were sending away using military force. When they realized that the Sinhalese sister was still in the community, they ordered that she leave immediately, or, if she didn't, they threatened to do something to their house. The Tamil-speaking sisters in the community refused to send her away. The Bishop, fearing for the lives of the sisters, advised them to send her to the South, at least for the time being. The others in the community, and the people of the neighborhood (Tamils), all wanted the sister to remain, saying that they would protect her. The provincial too agreed that she remain, and the sister herself wanted to remain, in spite of the risks involved. Days, weeks and months passed, and nothing happened. The situation improved, and the mission of Christ continued as usual. Above all, the community had succeeded in witnessing to extraordinary courage and gospel values in a war situation.

Choosing Peace in Papua New Guinea

The Mother of the Word Province of Franciscan Sisters made a commitment in November 2000 to try to live more fully the gospel values of nonviolent love. Their question was, "How to keep alive within each one of the members and others this dream of a world full of peace with no violence?" The sisters came up with two possibilities: 1) to develop skills for nonviolent living, and 2) to encourage groups to learn ways to live and practice nonviolence in order to challenge

43

systems in which ethnicity or class or wealth become divisive sources of injustice through nonviolent action. This theme has been adopted by the Federation of Religious of Papua New Guinea and in all regions, the men and women religious have become wholeheartedly involved.

The Franciscan Sisters contacted the Alternatives to Violence Project (AVP) in Australia. This is an international group committed to reducing violence by encouraging and training people in the use of creative nonviolent strategies. Now, members of religious orders are presenting their own workshops using a modified version of the AVP program. The learning is almost completely experiential, resulting in commitments to begin the journey into nonviolent living. They hope to extend the program to youth groups, staff groups in diocesan administration, counseling teams, family planning teams and to schools, both primary and secondary.

Reflection Question

What experiences in your own life, community and culture are examples of the challenges and possibilities of affirming "difference without division"?

3 Nonviolent Intervention, Encounter, and the Third Way: St. Francis and the Wolf of Gubbio

At a time when St. Francis was staying in the town of Gubbio, something wonderful and worthy of lasting fame happened. For there appeared in the territory of that city a fearfully large and fierce wolf which was so rabid with hunger that it devoured not only animals but even human beings. All the people in the town considered it such a great scourge and terror –because it often came near town– that they took weapons with them when they went into the country, as if they were going to war. Everyone in the town was so terrified that hardly anyone dared go outside the city gate.

While the Saint was there at that time, he had pity on the people and decided to go out to meet the wolf. But on hearing this the citizens said to him: "Look out, Brother Francis. Don't go outside the gate, because the wolf which has already devoured many people will certainly attack you and kill you!" But St. Francis placed his hope in the Lord Jesus Christ who is master of all creatures. Protected not by a shield nor helmet,

helmet, but arming himself with the Sign of the Cross, he bravely went out of the town with his companion....

Then, in the sight of many people who had come out, the fierce wolf came running with its mouth open toward St. Francis and his companion. The Saint made the Sign of the Cross toward it. The power of God checked the wolf and made it slow down and close its cruel mouth. Then, calling to it, St. Francis said: "Come to me, Brother Wolf. In the name of Christ, I order you not to hurt me or anyone." As soon as he gave it that order, it lowered its head and lay down at the Saint's feet, as though it had become a lamb.

St. Francis said to it as it lay in front of him: "Brother Wolf, you have done great harm in this region, and you have committed horrible crimes by destroying God's creatures without any mercy... You therefore deserve to be put to death just like the worst robber and murderer. Consequently everyone is right in crying out against you and complaining, and this whole town is your enemy. But, Brother Wolf, I want to make peace between you and them, so that they will not be harmed by you any more, and after they have forgiven you all your past crimes, neither human beings nor dogs will pursue you any more."

The wolf showed by moving its body and tail and ears and by nodding its head that it willingly accepted what the Saint had said and would observe it. So St. Francis spoke again: "Brother Wolf, since you are willing to make and keep this peace pact, I promise you that I will have the people of this town give you food every day as long as you live, so that you will never again suffer from hunger, for I know that whatever evil you have been doing was done because of the urge of hunger.

But, my Brother Wolf, since I am obtaining such a favor for you, I want you to promise me that you will never hurt any animal or [human being].

Will you promise me that?" The wolf gave a clear sign, by nodding its head, that it promised to do what the Saint asked. Then St. Francis said: "Brother Wolf, I order you, in the name of the Lord Jesus Christ, to come with me now, without fear, into the town to make this peace pact in the name of the Lord." And the wolf immediately began to walk along beside St. Francis, just like a very gentle lamb.

When the people saw this they assembled on the market place, where St. Francis said, "Listen, dear people. Brother Wolf...has promised me and has given me a pledge that he will make peace with you and will never hurt you if you promise also to feed him every day. And I pledge myself as bonds[person] for Brother Wolf that he will faithfully keep this peace pact."

Then all the people who were assembled there promised in a loud voice to feed the wolf regularly. And St. Francis said to the wolf before them all: "And you, Brother Wolf, do you promise to keep the pact, that is, not to hurt any animal or human being?" The wolf knelt down and bowed its head, and by twisting its body and wagging its tail and ears it clearly showed to everyone that it would keep the pact as it had promised. From that day, the people and the wolf kept the pact which St. Francis made.

Little Flowers of St. Francis of Assisi[26]

Reflection

The fangs of the wolf were real. The human beings he killed were real. The danger he posed to the town was real.

The fear that paralyzed the town of Gubbio was realistic. It was based on an actual, verifiable threat. It seemed eminently reasonable to fear the wolf and stay fearfully behind the city walls or, if one ventured out, to go out "as if one were going to war."

The problem was that the mutual threat both parties posed to one another did not resolve this conflict. Instead, that threat only worsened it. The town and the wolf were locked in a spiral of violence that seemed sensible, inevitable, and without recourse. What else could either party do but continue on its path of violence and counter-violence; a path that left both both sides resembling one another in their fear and ferocity?

Albert Camus wrote that the great challenge for the human person in the modern age was to be *neither* a victim *nor* an executioner. St. Francis, eight centuries before this French existentialist, proposed this "third way" to the town and the world. Both sides of this conflict had become simultaneously victim *and* executioner. The saint proposed this alternative not so much with his words as with his body. Rooted in the saving power of God, St. Francis crosses from one social setting to another in order to heal both.

From the point of view of the townspeople, Francis leaves the zone of presumed safety (but one saturated and paralyzed by fear) and crosses into a terrain of danger perceived to be a province of chaos and violence. From the point of view of the wolf, Francis is both another source of sustenance and another form of threat sent from the town that is making war on him. However, Francis's risky action –his form of nonviolent intervention– subverts the perspectives of both parties. He reveals to the town that a spiritually-grounded openness to the other can puncture the opaque veil of fear, revealing the "other" as both wounded and sacred, not simply destructive. He reveals to the wolf that the decision not to match ferocity with ferocity is confounding and disclosing of a different kind of power, power that unifes rather than threatens.

Grounded in the power of the nonviolent God, Francis's unilateral initiative breaks the cycle of violence by affirming his oneness with the wolf (by calling him "Brother"), by truthfully naming the violence perpetrated by the wolf (his attacks on the town), by analyzing the root causes of the violence (hunger), by proposing an accord that would meet the needs of both parties and lastly by bringing both parties to affirm this mutually beneficial pact, which Francis offers to vouch for personally. With this resolution, there has perhaps also been an amelioration of a situation that caused the wolf's hunger in the first place: the pressures of the growing human population of the Italian cities of the time.

This story depicts a dynamic we often confront in life: a very real threat provoking a counter-threat that reinforces a pattern or script which endlessly subverts the possibility for a just resolution. It also dramatizes a "third way" that creatively opens space for alternatives not previously seen or, if seen, not considered realistic. While it cannot promise success in every case, nonviolent peacemaking relentlessly pursues alternatives to the chronic impasse of dehumanization or destruction. It affirms the underlying connectedness between antagonists –no matter their differences, a conviction underscored in this story by the fact that this resolution is achieved between different species. This stresses Gandhi's vision centuries later of active nonviolence striving for "difference without division."

The town of Gubbio incorporated Francis's peacemaking in its institutional memory. For example, in the 1970s Gubbio declared itself a "nuclear-free zone" and its city officials have been active in many campaigns for peace.

CONTEMPORARY EXPERIENCES

Why Franciscans stayed in the Church of the Nativity in Bethlehem

For five weeks in the Spring of 2002, Franciscan women and men chose to stay within the besieged Church of the Nativity in Bethlehem as the Israeli/Palestinian conflict escalated. The brothers and sisters chose to stay during the conflict because they were in their own house and had nothing to fear either from Palestinians or Israelis. They felt a responsibility to be faithful guardians of this Holy Site, a mandate entrusted to the Franciscans by the Church and protected by international law. But the principal reason for staying was to help avoid a direct military confrontation between the armed parties on both sides, with the subsequent loss of life and damage to one of Christianity's most holy of places. Because of their openness and respect to both sides, the brothers and sisters were able to play an important mediator role in the ongoing search for a diplomatic and peaceful solution to the standoff.

Franciscan Peacemaking in Latin America

Franciscans have long experimented with this dynamic of nonviolent intervention, solidarity, and accompaniment. In Latin America, many Franciscans have been involved in human rights work. In the O.F.M. San Pablo Province in Colombia, friars have been organizing "democracy projects" and civic participation classes. On one occasion a few years ago, Br. Ed Dunn, O.F.M. reported that friars working in a rural village were threatened by the paramilitaries and so they left the area. Not long after this, paramilitaries assassinated many of the lay leaders of the community. In an emergency meeting, the Franciscan province decided that whenever friars were threatened in the future and had to be removed, they would be replaced by another group of friars. The policy of "permanent presence" is based on their desire to contribute to a reduction in the levels of violence and aggression against the people.

At the same time, Franciscan sisters in the Brazilian rainforest have helped carry on the work of assassinated labor leader Chico Mendez. They have been seeking to maintain the integrity of the ecosystem there and to defend the human and economic rights of native peoples.

Reflection Question

What experiences in your own life, community and culture are examples of the challenges and possibilities of engaging in nonviolent intervention for justice and peace?

4 Pluralism, Fundamentalism and Active Nonviolence: St. Francis's Meeting with the Sultan

The head of these brothers, who also founded the order, came into our camp. He was so inflamed with zeal for the faith that he did not fear to cross the lines to the army of our enemy. For several days he preached the Word of God to the Saracens and made a little progress. The Sultan, the ruler of Egypt, privately asked him to pray to the Lord for him, so that he might be inspired by God to adhere to that religion which most pleased God.

Jacques de Vitry, Letter VI of 1220[27]

Reflection

In 1212, Francis set out for Syria but was shipwrecked. The next year he headed for Morocco but because of grave illness got only as far as Spain. In 1219, Francis finally traveled to Egypt and was able to meet people of Islam. On his arrival in Egypt, Francis received permission to go to the front lines and enter Damietta to speak with Malik-al-Kamil, the Sultan of Egypt. Jaques de Vitry, who was the Bishop of Acre [modern-day Israel] at the time, writes that Saracens captured Francis who told them that he was a Christian and asked to be taken to the Sultan. When the Sultan recognized in Francis a man of God, he treated him gently and gave Francis hospitality for several days, listening carefully to all Francis had to say.

De Vitry says that the Sultan sent Francis back to the Christian camp, because he was afraid that Francis's preaching would convert his soldiers. Two other early accounts say that the Sultan was advised by his spiritual counselors that Francis should be killed. This the Sultan refused to do, and so asked Francis to leave for his own safety but first said to him, "Pray for me, that God may deign to reveal to me the law and the faith which is more pleasing to Him." The Sultan reportedly gave Francis a safe-conduct pass to visit areas in the Holy Land at the time off-limits to Christians.

This event is not a "brave pilgrimage" to the Holy Places, nor is it a "success" story in the sense of conversions to Christianity. "Francis set out to meet other believers who did not believe in the Incarnation; [he] did not go on a pilgrimage to buildings of stone, but to the hearts of others."[28]

Willingness to be changed by the experience of encounter with the other is a necessary aspect of nonviolence. That his encounter with the Sultan had a profound influence on Francis's spirituality and on his understanding of the mission of those who are called to live among people of Islam can be seen in his instructions to missionaries.[29] However, on his return to the brothers Francis was able to share little of what he had learned because the minds of Christians, including his brothers, were so closed to the peoples of Islam. The fiery accounts

53

of the first groups of friars who went to preach to, and convert, followers of Islam in Francis's day make rather clear the fact that Francis's instructions were not understood.

The encounter of the Christian and Islamic cultures of that time began and continued in the bloody clash of medieval warfare. Many Christians assumed that followers of Islam were serving the devil. Soldiers tried to wrest the "Holy Lands" from them; missionaries tried to save them from damnation. The Crusades brought these two quite distinct cultures together in a way that blurred the boundaries of both.

Today, religious traditions that have shaped human experience for centuries are impinging upon one another in ways that easily lead to misunderstandings. As Michael Hadley notes in *The Justice Tree: Multifaith Reflection on Criminal Justice*,[30] cultural tensions combined with the failure to foster justice lead to the international conflicts that we face today.

While faith traditions have far more to contribute to harmony than to conflict, fundamentalism provokes conflict among followers of different faith traditions. In our day, believers in these traditions are challenged to rethink bedrock assumptions about key values, such as: the nature of humanity, the uses of power and of violence, the resolution of human conflict. In this regard Francis's encounter with the Sultan has much to offer for a reflection on nonviolence. The recognition that truth is not the property of a single person or tradition –but can be found at the core of each person– is basic to nonviolence. The ability to listen respectfully, and to be willing to be changed by an aspect of truth expressed by another, is necessary to the practice of nonviolence. Francis and the Sultan witness to a willingness to search together for aspects of truth found in different traditions.

Practicing the disciplines of openness and reverence is part of active nonviolence. Entering into this kind of search calls us to move beyond simplistic and literal understandings of the teachings that ground our religious traditions. It calls for discerning study and dialogue, as well as contemplation and prayerful attention to Wisdom –the source of Life and of Truth. It calls, as well, for the courtesy that we see in both Francis and the Sultan in their encounter.

CONTEMPORARY EXPERIENCES
Life in Morocco

Franciscans have lived in Morocco since the time of St. Francis. Over the centuries one of the principal efforts has been to live respectfully as Friars Minor among Muslims. The emphasis is placed on presence and not on efforts to convert others to their religion. Besides building up mutual understanding and friendship, Franciscans try to contribute to the integral development of the Islamic people, especially by promoting educational and health projects. In Mecnes, the brothers live in the Medina, or the oldest part of the ancient city, in an apartment surrounded by the people. The people, especially the young, feel free to visit and be with the brothers, as well as use the library facilities, an excellent resource for their ongoing education. In Marrakech, a brother has helped promote an organization that advises Moroccan nongovernmental organizations on development projects. The organization is run by Moroccans themselves in a Franciscan house.

Franciscan Nonviolence in Asia: One Province

One of the Franciscan provinces in Asia which is practicing nonviolent resistance shall remain nameless to avoid creating difficulties for the brothers. The province's policy is to open up spaces for religious, social and political freedom. The friars do not criticize the government openly or use confrontational tactics to get their point across. They dialogue with the civil authorities, persist in trying to achieve their objectives (even when particular strategies fail), resist the temptation to use bribery, participate in local community organizations, contribute ideas, and when needed, constructively criticize without treating the adversary with contempt. The friars' social projects are mostly done in conjunction with the civil and political authorities. They do not simply wait for changes or new political structures, they avoid lamenting the fact that they do not live in the perfect society but rather they joyfully live their Franciscan vocation now. This approach recognizes that the political changes have been a grace for the church and in particular an opportunity for Franciscans to reappraise their original vocation and adjust accordingly.

Neve Shalom/Wahat al-Salam: Peacebuilding in Action

Neve Shalom/Wahat al-Salam is a community, a school, and a peacemaking project in Israel. An integrated community of Palestinians and Jews, Neve Shalom/Wahat al-Salam has brought Palestinians and Jews together to engage one another over the past two decades. Over the course of several days, the participants go through three phases of encounter. The first is the process of mutual discovery of the humanness of one another. The second is a searching reflection on the power differences between the groups –how, in spite of their humanization, generally speaking, the violence of structural injustice exists that must be addressed or there can never be true peace. Finally, the participants imagine thirty years forward into the future– and how they have to construct this future together. Neither community is going away –so it is up to them mutually and collaboratively to create a just and peaceful society together.

Reflection Question

What experiences in your own life, community and culture are examples of the challenges and possibilities of nonviolent engagement?

5 Active Nonviolence and Restorative Justice: The Three Robbers at Monte Casale

Now at that time three notorious robbers frequented the district, who committed many ill deeds there. One day they came to the place of the friars and sought out Friar Angelo, the guardian, that he would feed them, whereupon the guardian answered them in this manner, rebuking them harshly ... They were angry and left with indignation. At that moment St. Francis returned from being out. When the guardian had told him how he had driven those men away, St. Francis rebuked him severely, saying that he had acted cruelly, inasmuch as sinners are better called back to God by gentleness that by cruel reproofs... "Seeing then, that you have acted contrary to the Holy Gospel of Christ, I command you by obedience that you immediately take this wallet of bread which I have begged and this vessel of wine and seek them diligently until you find them. Then give them all this bread and wine in my name.

Afterward you must kneel down before them and humbly confess to them your sin of cruelty. Then pray them in my name to do evil no longer, but to fear God and offend Him no more. If they will do this, I promise to provide for their needs and to give them to eat and drink continually. When you have told them this, return here in a humble spirit."

While the guardian went to do what he commanded, St. Francis prayed and beseeched God that He would soften the hearts of those robbers and convert them to repentance. The obedient guardian came up with them and gave them the bread and wine and did and said what St. Francis had told him....

They went in haste to St. Francis and spoke to him thus, "Father, by reason of the many horrible sins which we have committed, we do not believe that we can turn to the mercy of God. But if you have any hope that God will receive us with mercy, indeed we are ready to do what you shall bid us and to do penance with you."

St. Francis received them lovingly and benignly and consoled them with many examples, assuring them of the mercy of God.

Little Flowers of St. Francis of Assisi[31]

Reflection

This story calls us again to certain aspects essential to Francis's practice of nonviolence: courtesy which disarms the heart; the fundamental motivation of loving as God loves and expressing that love in tangible and practical ways. As in the Gubbio story, he promises to provide food for them, realizing that most bandits robbed because they were hungry. He does this through the brothers whom he sends to find the robbers. His nonviolence is

59

practical, realistic and aims to take away the justification or reason for violence. His motives are not merely strategic. In the first place, he is wanting to follow Jesus' gospel way, and it happens that this is an effective way of nonviolent love.

Concepts fundamental to restorative justice are also illustrated in this story. It becomes obvious in the course of the story that Francis's nonviolent response comes from unconditioned and respectful regard. The way of acting with the robbers has nothing to do with what they have earned by their evil deeds. There is no thought of punishment, only of bringing them to the desire to repent and restoring them to community. And even repentance has nothing to do with punishment, but only with opening oneself to God's love and the love of others, which will turn our lives around if we give it the chance!

The model of restorative justice regards crime as a violation of people and relationships. Rather than placing an emphasis on punishment, it is concerned with healing the wounds of the victim, community and offenders alike. This model aims at ongoing transformation of perspectives, of structures and of persons. It is quite distinct from a retributive model, which has as its aim punishment for violations of law. Jim Considine, the national Coordinator of the New Zealand Restorative Justice Network, describes restorative justice as "a philosophy that moves from punishment to reconciliation, from vengeance against offenders to healing for victims, from alienation and harshness to community and wholeness, from negativity and destructiveness to healing, forgiveness and mercy."[32]

Restorative justice networks in many countries are working, with varying degrees of success, to bring a new awareness to civil society and to bring about structural changes in the criminal justice system. Efforts to establish truth and reconciliation commissions within nations/

regions that have been torn apart by repression and violent conflict also reflect this idea of restorative justice. A member of the South African Truth and Reconciliation commission, Pumla Gobodo-Madikizela, suggests that "[a] perpetrator's genuine apology could be the crucial moment that frees a victim who has felt burdened by years of bitterness and hate."[33]

CONTEMPORARY EXPERIENCE
Franciscan Messengers

A few years ago in a school in the predominantly Sinhalese area of Moratuwa, Sri Lanka, a Franciscan Missionary of Mary sister started an association among the school children called the Messengers of St. Francis. The members of this association meet regularly and search together how they could live the Franciscan values in the present context of the country. Last Christmas, they collected many useful gifts in the school and sent them to the people on the war-torn east coast region. They have also started corresponding with them. The students are all learning Tamil, and are now able to communicate and correspond in this language. Presently, they are organizing a meeting with some students on the east coast: they are sending the Tamil students an invitation to visit them in the South to break down barriers which had been built during the more than thirty years of an ethnic war. They hope to build new relationships of love and nonviolence, of understanding and appreciation between the two ethnic groups.

Peace Courts

On the Rosebud Lakota Reservation in South Dakota, USA, an Elder Legal Conference explored traditional methods of conflict resolution in order to develop a model of transformative mediation close to the spirit of traditional problem solving. They have now established a Peace Court and have trained the first group of mediators. Some of the trainees have indicated that the system truly resembles the *tiyospaye* model that had been used by the Lakota from time immemorial. They see it as a step forward in creating a Lakota social system, and a move that will help create bonds among the people. The Peace Court will offer all disputing parties the opportunity to sit down with a trained mediator to resolve differences as an alternative to handling their differences in a formal court of law.

Community members of an impoverished neighborhood in the U.S. city of San Francisco, California have been working toward a similar model of restorative justice. This neighborhood has been considered by civil and legal authorities as more a zone where crime could be contained rather than as a community. Community members call their restorative justice experiment the Community Court. The Community Court in this setting will actually help create community by bringing disputing residents together. Neighbors are trained in mediation to help resolve disputes in ways that do not diminish either party, but rather empower each party to find the resolution able to address the needs of all concerned.

Reflection Question

What experiences in your own life, community and culture are examples of the challenges and possibilities of restorative justice?

6 St. Clare and Relentless Persistence

The Lord of Ostia (Cardinal Protector, Reynaldus), after hearing about the increase of her sickness, hurried to visit the spouse of Christ. [He had become] a father [to her] by his office, a provider by his care, always a dedicated friend by his very pure affection. He nourished the sick [woman] with the Sacrament of the Body of the Lord, and fed [those] remaining with the encouragement of his salutary word.

Then she begged so great a father with her tears to take care of her soul and those of the other Ladies for the name of Christ. But, above all, she asked him to petition to have the Privilege of Poverty confirmed by the Lord Pope and the Cardinals.

Because he was a faithful helper of the Order, just as he promised by his work, so he fulfilled in deed.

Clare of Assisi: Early Documents[34]

Reflection

The story of Clare's Rule of Life is almost as long as her life in the community of Poor Ladies at San Damiano. Indeed, even after the rule that she wrote was approved, the one element excluded from the approbation was what was dearest to her: the "privilege of poverty." Finally, a few days before her death, the Pope himself visits her, grants and signs the approval of this life in radical poverty, without property.

Relationship, so fundamental to active nonviolence, calls the practitioner to engage the opponent with respect. Sister Briege O'Hare, O.S.C. describes a basic stance of Clare in this way: "finding God incarnate in every living thing and especially in the embrace of the totality of our own humanity and the humanity of our sisters and brothers even where, and especially where, we are most frail and vulnerable."[35] Such a stance is at the heart of engaging one's opponent with respect.

Clare had the ability to dialogue without losing sight of that to which she was called by God. This enabled Clare to persist in her campaign to have an appropriate Rule of Life for her and her sisters. Over the years she dealt with different Popes, as well as a Cardinal who eventually became Pope, in this question of the Rule. With each one she engaged in dialogue, shared the discernment of her sisters, their lived experience, their conviction of the path to which they were called. Though she and her sisters experimented with the guidance that was offered in the way of a Rule of Life, they also continued to listen to their experience and to the call they experienced. Then they would express anew their commitment to their form of life.

It is out of this experience that Clare guided another sister, Agnes of Prague, through a process of discerning her own response to authorities who wished to modify the way of life to which she felt called. Clare's second letter to Agnes outlines a process of discernment that could well be used as part of developing nonviolent action strategies. Gandhi, speaking of experiments in truth, described a similar process. The "staying power," or strength that supports long-term, relentless persistence to achieve nonviolent social change comes from drawing upon the wisdom of those who are involved in a particular situation, from thorough analysis of the situation and from the wisdom in one's faith tradition.

CONTEMPORARY EXPERIENCE
Journey to Reconciliation

Nonviolent processes leading to reconciliation generally unfold slowly. The willingness to persist for a lifetime, or to continue something that passes from one generation to another is crucial. We know that hatred can be carried over for many generations. Love also can be passed on, transforming generation after generation.

The story of Irene Laure is one example of this. Her work to reconcile French and German peoples after the Second World War was a major factor in the birth of a new postwar European culture. People who have never met her, who live far from Europe in another generation, have been influenced by her work and some processes of reconciliation have included elements drawn from the Franco-German reconciliation.

Irene, who, with her whole family, had been a member of the

French resistance to the Nazi occupation during World War II, learned to hate Germany and to long for its destruction. During a postwar conference in Switzerland, she came to the moment of struggling with that hatred and recognizing that hatred always causes new wars. At that conference, she was able to state publicly that she had come to realize that she was wrong for harboring this hatred; she asked forgiveness of the Germans there.

Her wholehearted entrance into the work of Franco-German reconciliation also meant entering into a journey of soul enabling her to love and esteem the German people who had suffered so much in the same war. She has come to be a model for the process of moving from a sense of victimhood with its accompanying violence, to becoming an advocate for renewal of the soul of a people.[36]

Confronting Nuclear Testing for Two Decades

In preparation for the 800th anniversary of the birth of Saint Francis in 1982, members of the Order of Friars Minor were asked to find ways to mark this significant commemoration. Franciscans of the Province of Santa Barbara (California, USA) joined with the Franciscan Sisters of Penance and Charity to highlight efforts to carry out Francis's mission of peace. One of the most notable of these was a forty-day Lenten witness at the Nevada Test Site during Lent 1982. The United States government has tested nuclear weapons for the past fifty years at the Nevada Test Site. A vigil was held every day at the entrance to the facility, inviting workers, scientists and the larger community to call a halt to nuclear weapons testing and to pray for an end to the arms race. Large numbers of peace seekers, including many Franciscans, assembled during Holy Week. Many fasted. On Good Friday participants engaged in the "Way of the Cross" up the road to the Test Site. In an act of nonviolent peacemaking, a large number of people crossed the boundaries onto the Nevada Test Site property and were arrested. The protest continued through a celebration on Easter morning of commitment to peacemaking and to ending nuclear testing.

Following this eighth centennial anniversary, the Nevada Desert Experience was formed to continue the active nonviolence at the Nevada Test Site. Many women and men were inspired to continue this witness together with their Franciscan sisters and brothers. They have continued to vigil and advocate for the ending of nuclear testing –as well as restoring to the Western Shoshone people their land taken from them to form the test site. Every year members of various religious denominations come to these events and continue the vigil. After years of activity and in association with many people and groups around the world, a moratorium on nuclear testing was declared by U.S. government in 1992. But limited testing continues, and the anti-nuclear movement continues to press for the end of *all* preparations for war at this site.

Many Franciscans, as well as people of other faiths and goodwill have seen this manifestation as a witness of Francis of Assisi in these times. He continues to inspire this peacemaking and reverence for all creation.

Reflection Question

What experiences in your own life, community and culture are examples of the challenges and possibilities of relentless persistence for peace, justice, and reconciliation?

7 Processes of Reconciliation: The Bishop and the Mayor

At that same time when [Francis] lay sick, the bishop of the city of Assisi at the time excommunicated the podestá [the mayor]. In return, the man who was then podestá was enraged, and had this proclamation announced, loud and clear, throughout the city of Assisi: no one was to sell or buy anything from the bishop, or to draw up any legal document with him. And so they thoroughly hated each other.

Although very ill, blessed Francis was moved to pity for them, especially since there was no one, religious or secular, who was intervening for peace and harmony between them. He said to his companions: "It is a great shame for you, servants of God, that the bishop and the podestá hate one another in this way, and that there is no one intervening for peace and harmony between them." And so, for that reason, he composed one verse for the Praises:

Praised be you, my Lord, through those who give pardon
for your love, and bear infirmity and tribulation.
Blessed are those who endure in peace for by you, Most High,
they shall be crowned.

Afterwards he called one of his companions and told him: "Go to the podestá and on my behalf, tell him to go to the bishop's residence together with the city's magistrates and bring with him as many others as he can."

And when the brother had gone, he said to two of his other companions: "Go and sing the Canticle of Brother Sun before the bishop, the podestá, and the others who are with them. I trust in the Lord that he will humble their hearts and they will make peace with each other and return to their earlier friendship and love."

When they had all gathered in the piazza inside the cloister of the bishop's residence, the two brothers rose and one of them said:

"In his illness, blessed Francis wrote the Praises of the Lord for His creatures, for His praise and the edification of his neighbor. He asks you, then, to listen to them with great devotion." And so, they began to sing and recite to them. And immediately the podestá stood up and folding his arms and hands with great devotion, he listened intently, even with tears, as if to the gospel of the Lord. For he had a great faith and devotion toward blessed Francis.

When the Praises of the Lord were ended, the podestá said to everyone: "I tell you the truth, not only do I forgive the lord bishop, whom I must have as my lord, but I would even forgive one who killed my brother or my son." And so he cast himself at the lord bishop's feet, telling him: "Look, I am ready to make amends to you for everything, as it pleases you, for the love of our Lord Jesus Christ and of his servant Francis."

Taking him by the hands, the bishop stood up and said to him: "Because of my office humility is expected of me, but because I am naturally prone to anger, you must forgive me." And so, with a great kindness and love they embraced and kissed each other.

...All the others who were present and heard it took it for a great miracle, crediting it to the merits of blessed Francis.

Francis of Assisi: Early Documents[37]

Reflection

Despite the physical suffering he experienced toward the end of his life, Francis was happy after composing the *Canticle of Creation*. But, as Arnaldo Fortini reports, this feeling soon dissipated: "He was shaken out of that ecstatic mood by a new war...Assisi went to war with Perugia again."[38] The Pope had tried to stop the war by threatening anyone with excommunication who entered into alliances compelling them to go to war with another city or party. But the battle went forward. "Everyone rose up ferociously against his neighbor. The walls oozed fraternal blood. Those inside the city were subjected to hunger, and those outside, to never-ending slaughter...the *podestá* [mayor] of Assisi swore on his part to observe the new agreements [alliances]. It was an open challenge to the pope and the Papal State. Bishop Guido excommunicated the *Podestá.*"[39] Guido's sentence of excommunication made the mayor rise up in fury. To his eyes and those of the other city people, the imperious bishop was the eternal adversary of the commune, the enemy in the house."[40] Fortini describes the violent responses: "Murderous deeds forming a strange contrast to the canticle of love that was coming from San Damiano... In [Mayor] Oportulo's proclamations we know their bloody terroristic acts...And the same bitter feeling that drove these violent men was shared...by the bishop."[41]

We are aware from these citations that we are not dealing with a misunderstanding or argument between the Bishop and the Mayor. There are serious structural challenges involving the nobility, the new merchant class, the commune and the Church. Basically, in the language of theologian and biblical scholar Walter Wink in *Engaging the Powers*, we are dealing with struggles within the domination system. Who will be in control: the powerful factions of the commune or the people allied with the pope? Wink insists that there are Powers that belong to these institutions that enforce domination and preclude peaceful resolution. "What people in the world of the Bible experienced and called 'Principalities and Powers' was in fact real," Wink writes. "They were discerning the actual spirituality at the center of the political, economic and cultural institutions of their day."[42] "I use the expression 'the Domination System'," Wink explains, "to indicate what happens when an entire network of Powers becomes integrated around idolatrous values."[43]

Wink continues: "Any attempt to transform a social system without addressing both its spirituality and its outer forms is doomed to failure." Francis seemed to have an intuitive understanding of this. While fully aware of the demonic nature of the institutions of his times that caused such bloodshed, poverty and suffering, he also addressed the deeper spiritual disease, the thirst for violence, the lack of a sense of reverence for God's creatures, and the failure to appreciate the gift of creation.

Wink holds that "The Powers are good [created by God]. The Powers are fallen. The Powers must be redeemed." While recognizing the demonic in each of the institutions involved, Francis also acknowledged the source of their creation and sought to restore them to the God-given purpose for which they were created. He did this through example, through intervention and through bestowing God's grace and peace. Francis lived in a world of violence, sometimes referred to as "redemptive violence," which claimed that order over chaos was brought about by violence. Into this world of enormous violence, Francis introduces a culture of nonviolence and helps brings about a state of peace. Wink sees the gospel as the alternative power to the Domination System.[44] Francis brings this gospel alternative to new life in the world.

As the story notes, Francis is pained to see that no one intervened to reestablish peace and concord. So he accepted the call of the Beatitudes to be a "peacemaker." Francis called upon his enormous political capital (goodwill among the powers) to intervene. Bishop Guido had played a major role in the birth and development of the Franciscan movement. The *podestá* was among Francis's most devoted supporters. His daughter Agnes had joined Clare at San Damiano at an early age. Oportulo treasured the memory. Both the bishop and the mayor held Francis in the highest esteem.

Francis uses a subtle approach of nonviolence. He adds another strophe to his *Canticle of the Creatures*. He sends one of his brothers to call the podestá to go to the bishop's palace, and another to prepare the bishop. Francis did not go but remained in prayer. He then calls upon the brothers to sing to those assembled his song. "A wish for peace has been his greeting to them. It may be his last affectionate word."[45] According to the story, the mayor and the bishop were moved to great repentance and a mutual embrace.

Fortini notes that "In this moment [at least], a centuries-old struggle for power ends... The people...say that Francis has wrought a miracle."[46] Fortini credits this intervention with bringing about a true peace. Others credit the lay Franciscans who by their state refused to bear arms. Pope Gregory IX attested that through Francis's influence peace came to this part of the world.

Wink was involved in the nonviolent movement to overcome the vicious apartheid system in South Africa. He has written about the unexpected nonviolent transformation of the former Soviet Union and other places around the world of the past several decades. One key dimension of these changes was prayer and prayerful action. Wink believes that the future belongs to the intercessors.

Wink asserts that prayer is the most important discipline. It is the means by which we engage the Powers and achieve victory. Prayer gives God the openness to enter into the world and achieve a transformation. Intercession visualizes an alternative future to the one created by the momentum of current forces. History belongs to the intercessors who believe the future into being. And the world changes.

Francis offers us a good example of the intercessor who created a different future. We see this exemplified by Francis, who prayed in his cell while the brothers engaged the opposing powers with the gentleness of Francis's song. He continues to inspire Franciscans to activate a new future through their prayers today. This special role of the Second Order, the Poor Clares, was surely recognized by Clare and her sisters. Their presence in many of the areas of conflict today validate the significance of their prayer.

CONTEMPORARY EXPERIENCE
Nonviolence in a Time of War

Fr. Odorico D'andrea was the parish priest of San Rafael del Norte, located in Jinotega, Nicaragua from the year 1954 to his death in 1990. A creative and dynamic friar, he was known for his piety and his multiple works in favor of the poor of the area. Many of the facilities now enjoyed by the people – roads, bridges, houses, schools, hospitals and even a Sanctuary to Our Lady of Guadalupe– were initiated and carried to completion by him. The spacious church in honor of San Rafael is a permanent reminder of his presence.

But the most interesting examples of his commitment to peace are to be found during the years 1982 through 1988 when the area was the scene of constant battles between the Sandinista army and the Contra rebels in the mountains. Fr. Odorico struggled ceaselessly to bring peace among the warring factions. He was respected by both groups and maintained communication with the commanding officers in an effort to lessen the suffering of the people. He sought those who had been kidnapped or co-opted by either group and tried to help the warring groups see the others' humanity in whatever way possible. It was not uncommon to see a Russian officer (military advisors to the Sandinistas) among the people waiting to consult with him when he returned in the evenings from his pastoral visits to the country villages.

Perhaps Fr. Odorico is best known for the Mass for Peace which he organized one day in the mountains of Jinotega with the presence of the two warring factions facing each other in a line over their rifles which were placed on the ground. At the moment for offering the sign of peace he persuaded the men of each group to lean over the rifles and extend their hand to the "enemy." Only the strong personality and prayer of Fr. Odorico could have brought about such a celebration in the middle of the war. For this and many other actions in favor of the people he will be long remembered, not only by the people of the area, but by the entire population of Nicaragua.

Dialogue in the Desert

"The main thing is not to fear approaching anyone," says Sister Rosemary Lynch, O.S.F. "We need to learn to approach those whom we or others regard as enemies... If we can possibly imbibe a little of the spirit of Saint Francis, it will help...We need to approach those we are trained to hate or resent or fear, and to do it on a human level, in a very loving way, seeing them as Francis saw the Sultan, as a brother given to him by God. If we can do that, what can we not accomplish?"[47]

In the 1980s while U.S. and British nuclear weapons were frequently detonated at the Nevada Test Site, Sr. Rosemary met with General Mahlon Gates, the director of the facility. While many protestors demonstrated outside the nuclear test site, Sister Rosemary insisted that it was essential also to engage the opponent in dialogue. In 1982, she was able to arrange a private meeting with General Gates.

In doing this, Sister Rosemary was following Mohandas Gandhi's

Pace e Bene Nonviolence Service

stress on the necessity of dialogue. Her action likewise echoed the spirit of Francis in his engagement with the Sultan. Francis's goal was not to force submission but to change the heart of the opponent. Although General Gates did not become converted to end nuclear testing, he and Sr. Rosemary prayed together and helped sow the seeds of peace. Their relationship helped create an environment in which, over the next two decades, thousands of peacemakers would journey to the test site to pray for peace. This ongoing activity played an important role in creating the conditions for a moratorium on nuclear testing honored by most of the world's nuclear nations.

A Friar And The Mayor Visit Two Presidents

There have been several recent efforts to embody Francis's mission of peace. One example has been the work of Friar Gianmaria Polidori, the Custos of the Basilica of *Santa Maria degli Angeli,* where the early friars lived and where St. Francis died. Joining with the mayor of Assisi and other seekers of peace, Friar Gianmaria has visited various heads of state. In the 1980s they met with President Ronald Reagan of the United States and President Mikhael Gorbachev of the Soviet Union, prior to Gorbachev's call for domestic reforms within the U.S.S.R. (*perestroika*) and a new relationship with the West *(glasnost).*

President Reagan traveled to Europe to meet with President Gorbachev again. Before leaving the U.S., Reagan announced that he would not be "taken in" by Gorbachev, whom he likened to Darth Vader, the evil antagonist of the *Star Wars* movie. Yet when the two presidents met, they engaged in a serious discussion about how to make the world safer. They agreed to initiate a disarmament process known as "zero option." This would mean an end of all nuclear weapons. They later moderated this, but we were set on the way to greater nuclear disarmament. With many other efforts around the world, the peace mission of the Franciscans from Assisi and the prayers of the faithful contributed to creating the conditions for arms control agreements reached during the 1980s.

At that time, the people-to-people diplomacy movement emerged, expressing an insistent and popular demand for peace. Thousands of individuals and groups crossed national and international boundaries, providing a kind of mediation which governments were unable or unwilling to create. This people-to-people movement continues today.

Reflection Question

What experiences in your own life, community and culture are examples of the challenges and possibilities of love and reconciliation in action?

PART 2

Resources for Active and Transformative Nonviolence

The Decalogue for a Spirituality of Franciscan Nonviolence

Transformative nonviolence calls us to:

1. Learn to recognize and respect *"the sacred"* ("that of God" as the Quakers say) in every person, including in ourselves, and in every piece of Creation. The acts of the nonviolent person help to free this *Divine* in the opponent from obscurity or captivity.

2. Accept oneself deeply, "who I am" with all my gifts and richness, with all my limitations, errors, failings and weaknesses, and to realize that I am accepted by God. To live in the truth of ourselves, without excessive pride, with fewer delusions and false expectations.

3. Recognize that what I resent, and perhaps even detest, in another, comes from my difficulty in admitting that this same reality lives also in me. To recognize and renounce my own violence, which becomes evident when I begin to monitor my words, gestures, reactions.

4. Renounce dualism, the "We/They" mentality (Manicheism). This divides us into "good people/bad people" and allows us to demonize

the adversary. It is the root of authoritarian and exclusivist behavior. It generates racism and makes possible conflicts and wars.

5. Face fear and to deal with it, not mainly with courage but with love.

6. Understand and accept that the *New Creation*, the building up of the *Beloved Community* is always carried forward with others. It is never a "solo act." This requires patience and the ability to pardon.

7. See ourselves as a part of the whole creation to which we foster a relationship of love, not of mastery, remembering that the destruction of our planet is a profoundly spiritual problem, not simply a scientific or technological one. *We are one.*

8. Be ready to suffer, perhaps even with joy, if we believe this will help liberate the *Divine* in others. This includes the acceptance of our place and moment in history with its trauma, with its ambiguities.

9. Be capable of celebration, of joy, when the presence of God has been accepted, and when it has not been to help discover and recognize this fact.

10. Slow down, to be patient, planting the seeds of love and forgiveness in our own hearts and in the hearts of those around us. Slowly we will grow in love, compassion and the capacity to forgive.

By Rosemary Lynch, O.S.F. and Alain Richard, O.F.M.

Martin Luther King, Jr.'s Principles of Nonviolence

1) Nonviolence is a way of life for courageous people.
- It is active nonviolent resistance to evil.
- It is assertive spiritually, mentally and emotionally.

2) Nonviolence seeks to win friendship and understanding.
- The end result of nonviolence is redemption and reconciliation.
- The purpose of nonviolence is the creation of the Beloved Community.

3) Nonviolence seeks to defeat injustice, not people.
- Nonviolence holds that evil doers are also victims.
- The nonviolent resister seeks to defeat evil, not people.

4) Nonviolence holds that voluntary suffering can educate and transform.
- Nonviolence accepts suffering without retaliation.
- Nonviolence accepts violence if necessary, but will never inflict it.
- Nonviolence willingly accepts the consequences of its acts.
- Unearned voluntary suffering is redemptive and has tremendous educational and transforming possibilities.
- Voluntary suffering can have the power to convert the enemy when reason fails.

5) Nonviolence chooses love instead of hate.
- Nonviolence resists violence of the spirit as well as the body.
- Nonviolent love gives willingly, even knowing that it might face hostility.
- Nonviolent love is active, not passive.
- Nonviolent love is unending in its ability to forgive in order to restore community.
- Nonviolent love does not sink to the level of the hater.
- Love for the enemy is how we demonstrate love for ourselves.
- Love restores community and resists injustice.
- Nonviolence recognizes the fact that all life is interrelated.

6) Nonviolence believes that the universe is on the side of justice.
- The nonviolent resister has deep faith that justice will eventually win.
- Nonviolence believes that God is a God of justice and love.

This summary of M.L. King, Jr.'s principles was adapted by the Fellowship of Reconciliation from King's book Stride Toward Freedom (New York: Harper & Row, 1958).

Putting Transformative Nonviolence Into Practice: A Four-Step Process of Conflict Resolution

1. Centering Ourselves

When we find ourselves facing violence, injustice, or other conflicts, it is important to remain in our true selves. Otherwise, we are a prisoner of our roles, including the role where we feel justified to use violence against ourselves or others.

One way to do this is to is to experience what facilitators Maureen Gatt and Gerald Hair call our "Inner Observer," the reality within us which is contemplatively and lovingly present and watching. We are invited to return to that grounded reality and to act from that place –where we are most truly ourselves. In order to do this, we ask ourselves, "What am I feeling? What is the larger picture? Where is God in this situation?" We also take time to center ourselves and thus to decide what we should do in the situation at hand.

By anchoring ourselves in our deepest reality, we are prepared to respond –and not simply to react– to the conflict we are facing. We may decide to protect ourselves. We may decide to engage. In either case, we can act from that place where we are most truly who we are, and not simply from a worn out and potentially destructive script.

2. Disclosing Our True Selves-To Ourselves and to Our Opponent

This means first discovering what I am truly feeling in the situation, and then articulating those feelings to the one with whom I am in conflict. Am I feeling anger? Is there sadness or hurt or fear underneath this anger?

Second, this involves conveying these feelings to the one with whom we are in conflict. In other words, to share our heart more than our "position" or our "arguments." We should do this not in a way that "hits" the other person, but in a way that tries to get across who we really are in this moment.

85

3. Receiving the Truth of the Opponent

This may not be my truth, but it is theirs, and we will get nowhere until we both hear each other. It is also a way of acknowledging the other. As conflict resolution specialist Marshall Rosenberg puts it, *acknowledging* does not necessarily mean *agreeing*. We don't have to agree with their position —or the interests that lie below those positions— but we can acknowledge the other person and her or his truth.

4. Making Agreements, not Assumptions

By disclosing ourselves and listening to the other, we have a chance to discover the truth and untruth of the situation. We then have the basis for making agreements about how we are going to be with one another, rather than making assumptions. Many conflicts grow out of widely differing assumptions.

These four steps of active nonviolence are adapted from the work of activist and author, Bill Moyer and his workshop, "Moving From Dominating Behavior to Intimacy." Quoted in Ken Butigan with Patricia Bruno, O.P., From Violence To Wholeness *(Pace e Bene, 2002), pp. 43-44.*

Daily Practices to Cultivate Franciscan Nonviolence

Transformative nonviolence is a process of bringing us back to our truest selves. Ultimately, its techniques and strategies must draw their life from the well of sacredness within. Practically speaking, this means consciously cultivating those dimensions planted by God deep within our being, which bring life to ourselves, to other human beings, as well as to the earth and all its inhabitants. Now more than ever, our spiritual disciplines must deepen in us the vision and methods of nonviolent transformation. To this end, we are called to cultivate the spiritual dimensions of the nonviolent life on a daily basis. Here are some spiritual qualities that lie at the foundation of a spirituality of nonviolence, plus some suggestions for practicing them.

Awe

Often we are so absorbed in our everyday life that we assume that this is all there is. We come to believe that the structure and horizon of the world we experience –at home, in the work-place, and through the media– is "reality." By making this assumption, we often miss the fact that this social reality is *constructed* –it is a system of rules, beliefs and motivations that shape and limit our view of life. We tend, therefore, to overlook the fact that life is much more mysterious and unfathomable

87

than the systems we manufacture to navigate through the world. As theologian Karl Rahner, S.J. held, these systems are like tiny islands floating on a vast sea of mystery. When we cultivate a sense of awe for the great and irreducible mystery of our lives, we are able to see that life is more than the systems in which we live. We are also able to see that those systems can and must be transformed when they contradict or offend the great mystery of God that is our beginning and end.

One way of exploring this sense of mystery is to reflect on our encounters with other persons. On the one hand, these exchanges can be like following an agreed-upon formula. In that case, we are often like two billiard balls knocking against each other. On the other hand, our encounters with others can be experiences of deep communion. They can be holy moments where presence receives presence, experiences where, as phenomenologist Emmanuel Levinas says in *Totality and Infinity*, there is a "flow of infinity between one another's eyes." When two subjects encounter one another in this way –giving but not being destroyed, belonging but not "belonging to"– they experience in a momentary but tangible way the "ground of all being," the inexhaustible mystery which creates, preserves and embraces us.

One way of cultivating this sense of awe and mystery is to take some time in a quiet place and call to mind a very important encounter you had with another person. After imagining this event in detail, consider how it happened and what some of its consequences were. Notice your feelings as you remember this event. Reflect on the ways that this exchange had an unpredictable quality, a sense of possibility, transcending prescribed social ritual or conventional scripts. Sense the mystery of the situation. Reflect on how this mystery comes in part from the way that the depth dimension of both people was shared. This depth dimension or inner mystery is that aspect of us that cannot be reducible to our assumptions, expectations or systems. Throughout the day, cultivate an awareness of this mystery.

Gratitude

A nonviolent stance is one of deep gratefulness for our life and for all life. It is a posture which acknowledges the source of this life. It recognizes that each one of us is on a spiritual journey and that all of our experiences –happy or sad– teach and transform us. It salutes all the ways we have been gifted by God, our family, our teachers, our friends. One way of cultivating gratitude is taking some time in a quiet place and recalling ten people who have given of themselves so that your life could be better. Call to mind their faces. Remember in some detail what they have done for you. Recall the ways people have lavished their time, energy and resources on you. Then consider how God has lavished God's presence on you and on our world. Cultivate this awareness throughout the day, increasingly acknowledging how our entire life –and everything that passes through it– is a gift.

Receptivity

How do we cultivate our openness to those around us? One way is to practice letting go of the ego's armor in order to receive and heal the world. Here is an exercise which you can practice in the morning before leaving for work, or at any other time of the day.

Stand up, dropping your arms to your sides. Allow your entire body to relax. Breathe in God's grace; breathe it out into the world. Then slowly raise your arms and cross them in front of your eyes. Feel yourself protected and guarded. Slowly extend your arms outward in an attitude of openness to the world. After a few moments, move them in a gesture embracing the world. Repeat several times. This ritual can be performed alone or with others.

Compassion

Active nonviolence opens us to the two fundamental dimensions of all beings: sacredness and woundedness. It teaches us to share the suffering of others, as well as their fulfillment. Active nonviolence seeks to put this form of accompaniment into practice as each opportunity arises.

One way of cultivating compassion is to imagine someone with whom you have an unresolved conflict or unresolved negative feelings. Imagine them sitting in front of you. Look into her or his eyes. Share your feelings about this conflict with this person. Then ask her or him to speak. You may want to write down the "dialogue" that unfolds between you. Finish this encounter by praying for one another. (For more information about journal writing, see Ira Progoff's *At a Journal Workshop: The Basic Text and Guide for Using the Intensive Journal Process* [New York: Dialogue House Library, 1975]).

Joy

The horrors of this world are often overwhelming. Though these are not to be ignored, awe, gratitude, receptivity and compassion demand nothing less than engaging them fully. Horror is not the *ultimate* reality. Active nonviolence is a spiritual path that cultivates a keen awareness that *the meaning of life is found by joining wholeheartedly in God's joy.* How do we join in this divine rejoicing? We do this by letting it flow into all parts of our existence, including our modest efforts to mend the brokenness of our world.

We can cultivate this on a daily basis by becoming quiet and imagining God laughing. Go deeply into this laughter, into its roots –into that place where God declares that creation is good, that its inhabitants are good, that life is good.

Let us recall the words of Julian of Norwich: "The worst has already happened –and it has been repaired!"

Excerpted from: Ken Butigan with Patricia Bruno, O.P., From Violence to Wholeness (Berkeley, CA: Pace e Bene Nonviolence Service, 2002), pp. 51-53.

The Relationship between Trauma and the Practice of Active and Transformative Nonviolence

In a world fraught with violence at every level, trauma has become a commonplace experience. It has become such a part of our everyday experience that it often goes unrecognized. Sometimes the violence is directly experienced by individuals or groups. Often it has not been a direct experience, but the media's repeated images and reports of violence have so focused our thoughts that we are vicariously affected. Even our fear of violence, if excessive and unprocessed, can become a source of trauma.

The practice of active nonviolence calls for a calm, relaxed and alert stance, which enables the practitioner to respond with flexibility and creativity to a variety of experiences, including those that threaten the safety of those involved. When trauma goes unrecognized, within a person or group, the practice, the embodiment of nonviolence is difficult –sometimes not possible.

Francis's story of perfect joy is a helpful illustration. Francis and others are on the road on a cold rainy night. Thinking aloud, he imagines a scenario in which they arrive at their hermitage and the brothers do not recognize them or let them in but rather send them away in the darkness with only harsh words. Francis further imagines an amazing response. What if the cold and wet brothers respond with patience, even with unconditional loving regard for those who treat them so badly! Discovering such a response within oneself, Francis declares, would be perfect joy!

People who have experienced the healing of trauma, as well as the ability to respond to startling or even threatening situations in a calm manner, with mind and heart connection intact, have actually described feelings of joy, or of calm and deep happiness, even in the midst of difficult experiences.

In his very helpful book about the healing of trauma, *Waking the Tiger*, Peter A. Levine, Ph.D. points out that excessive caution and inhibitions, the need for ever-tightening circles of protection, compulsive re-enactment of traumatic experiences, victimization and unwise exposure to danger are often due to unresolved trauma. Whenever people cannot overcome the anxiety resulting from instinctive responses to past traumatic experiences, the consequence will be feelings of failure and betrayal by those who try to help. He suggests that until we understand that the symptoms of trauma are physiological as well as psychological, we will be hard pressed to resolve them.

Widespread work with groups and communities of people in the aftermath of war, political or criminal violence and natural disasters has brought about many discoveries helpful in dealing with the physiological symptoms of trauma.

Traumatic symptoms are not caused by the "triggering" event or situation but rather flow from the frozen energy that remains trapped in our nervous system, sometimes for years after the traumatic experience. The symptoms of trauma –feeling jumpy, panic reactions, flash-backs, exhaustion, and so on– form out of the residue of this frozen energy.

In fact, humans have the ability to engage this energy and release it, thus transforming the trauma and opening up new potential for creativity and wisdom. Fortunately, many ways of engaging and releasing these energies are being discovered and developed today. In our experience, the ability to engage and release the energy generated by past experiences (to process energy generated by present experiences) is key to developing the capacity for calm, relaxed and focused behavior necessary in the practice of active nonviolence.

A Sample Agenda for a Two-Hour Gathering to Reflect on Violence and Transformative Nonviolence

Processes of compassionate listening in the wake of violence are increasingly seen as a necessary step toward peace and reconciliation. The following model, developed by Pace e Bene Nonviolence Service, has been used in the wake of large-scale violence. It can be adapted for a variety of situations in order to provide a process for people to reflect on violence and active nonviolence in light of their feelings and their faith traditions. Creating space to make contact with our core truths after these wrenching events can help us touch the depth of this experience, encouraging wise and compassionate steps for mending our spirits and our broken world.

Welcome - 5 min.

Welcome people to this gathering. Explain that the goal is to open space for us to reflect prayerfully on the particular violence affecting us. We seek to create a safe and comfortable space so we can share what we are feeling, even if we disagree with one another. We seek to honor every person's perspective. This reflects the conviction that, by creating a place where our deepest feelings can be expressed and acknowledged in a respectful way, we open the possibility of coming to new wisdom and direction.

Share any housekeeping information needed for this gathering.

Opening Ritual, A Reading, and Introductions - 15 min.

Arrange the participants' chairs in a circle. Put a small table at the center. Place a small candle (and matches) for each person on the table. Use an audiocassette or compact disc with appropriate music. Invite people to stand and hold their arms out wide in front of them in a circle. Ask them to breathe in deeply and, while doing so, to slowly draw their arms in so their fingertips touch. Then, ask them to breathe out slowly, widening their arms back out. While they are doing this, ask them to breathe in the power of life and to breathe out all that hinders this power. Repeat this cycle four times. Then ask people to sit down.

Next ask the participants to symbolically bring their entire selves to the "altar": their sacredness and their woundedness; pieces of their truth and pieces of their "un-truth." Invite them to light a candle and, as they do so, to share a word, name or image that strikes them as appropriate. When everyone has finished, explain that we will draw on the wisdom of Judaism, Christianity, Islam and Buddhism in illuminating our reflection. We will begin with the following reading from the *Book of Wisdom*, Chapter 6: 12-14: "Wisdom is bright, and does not grow dim. By those who love her she is readily seen, and found by those who look for her. Quick to anticipate those who desire her, she makes herself known to them.

Watch for her early and you will have no trouble; you will find her sitting at your gates."

Ask people to introduce themselves.

Shared Agreements - 10 min.

Explain that we are seeking to make this gathering as safe as possible. In this spirit, ask for agreement on the following guidelines [photocopy the agreements ahead of time; distribute them so that people can read them silently as you read them aloud]:

1. I agree to share at whatever level I feel safe and comfortable

If you choose not to share, that's fine. If you want to share a little, that's fine. If you want to share more, that's fine. As the facilitator, I am not acting in the capacity of a professional psychotherapist. Together, we are ordinary people exploring the challenges of terrorism and war. We invite you to consult a psychotherapist or pastoral counselor if something comes up for you that you think warrants contacting an appropriate health professional.

2. I agree to honor confidentiality in my small group and in the large group

We ask that you not share something that has been shared with you unless you have been given permission to do so.

3. I agree to make our time together as safe, comfortable, and participatory as possible. I will do my best to:

Use "I" statements; support everyone's right to speak; listen actively; be conscious of non-verbal communication; show respect to others; practice cultural sensitivity; honor agreements about time; demonstrate patience; not interrupt others; maintain honesty; model openness; and show compassion.

Take a few minutes to discuss these agreements. If there is a question about the meaning of specific agreements, ask the large group to reflect on what they mean. Then ask the group for consensus about agreements.

Second Reading - 5 min.

As we begin our process, invite people to hear with their whole being the words of Jesus in The Gospel of Matthew, Chapter 5, verses 43-46: "You have heard it said, 'You must love your neighbor but hate your enemy.' But I say this to you: Love your enemies and pray for those who persecute you; in this way you will be children of God in heaven, for God causes the sun to rise on the bad as well as the good, and the rain to fall on the honest and dishonest alike."

Four Steps in the Journey from Violence to Wholeness in a Time of Crisis - 5 min.

Share the following: There are many steps in this journey. We want to suggest four of them. *First,* to center ourselves and get in touch with our "truest self" at this moment. *Second,* to disclose our truest self in this moment –to ourselves and to others. *Third,* to receive the truth of others. *Fourth,* to make agreements, not assumptions. We will briefly experiment with these steps, by first forming small groups to reflect on our "truest selves" in light of the current situation. [For more detail, see "Putting Transformative Nonviolence Into Practice: A Four-Step Process of Conflict Resolution" in this book.]

Journaling And Visualizing - 15 min.

Invite people to take some quiet time to express in words or images what they are feeling or experiencing in light of the current situation. This helps articulate their "truest selves" in this moment -- what we are really feeling (anger, grief, equanimity, etc.), plus our deepest longings for ourselves and the world. Provide people with notebook paper and pens as well as blank paper and crayons or colored markers. People can stay where they are sitting or go to some other space in the room or nearby. After 15 minutes, call people back for the next step.

Small Group Reflection - 15 min.

Form people into groups of three. Invite them, for example, to get together with those wearing articles of clothing that have a same or similar color, etc. Ask them –at whatever level they feel comfortable– to share their "truest selves" in light of this current situation. This could include sharing their journaling or drawing, though only voluntarily. Ask people to respect each person as she or he shares, even if they do not agree with them. After 15 minutes, call people back to the large group.

Large Group Reflection - 15 min.

Take a moment of silence to honor what has been shared. Then ask –again at whatever level they feel comfortable– if people would share with the large group what came up for them in the small groups. Afterward, read the Third Reading: *The Qur'an,* Chapter Four, verse 114: "Those who enjoin charity or justice or reconciliation among people –whoever does that, seeking the pleasure of God, will be given a great reward."

Role-Play - 20 min.

Ask people to form two parallel lines facing each other. Each person is asked to role-play a "nonviolent engagement" with the person directly across from her or him. One line represents people on one side of an important issue; the other represents people on the other side. Ask people in each line to turn around, close their eyes and really get into their role. But just before they start, ask them to consider the person they will be facing *with the same regard as the dearest, most important person in her or his life.* Then invite them to turn around and engage one another. After approximately three minutes, ask people to stop. Reflect with people on their feelings and experiences.

After a few minutes of group reflection, repeat the role-play, but with people taking the opposite position (i.e., the line in favor now becomes opposed, and vice versa). *Again, ask people to regard their "opponent" as the dearest, most important person in their life.* Then return to sitting in the large group and debrief this exercise; reflect on assumptions at work and whether there were any agreements.

Where Are We Being Called? - 5 min.

Ask people to turn to their neighbor and to reflect on any new insights or awarenesses –including new ways of seeing– that might have come up for them, as well as possible next steps on their own journey in light of the current situation.

Closing Circle - 5 min.

Form a circle and ask people to share a word that comes to mind as we close our time together. Before ending this event, share this reading from the Metta Sutra of Buddhism: "Even as a mother at the risk of her life watches over and protects her only child, so with a boundless mind should one cherish all living things, suffusing love over the entire world, above, below, and all around, without limit; so let one cultivate an infinite good toward the whole world."

Thank people for attending!

Lessons from Experience

Becoming Peacemakers: Reflections on Negotiating Peace

By Archbishop Thomas Menamparampil
Archdiocese of Guwahati, India

In the Kuki-Paite clashes in Manipur, India in 1997, some 400 people lost their lives, hundreds of villages were put to fire, and thousands of people were rendered homeless. That violent struggle lasted several months. We succeeded in holding peace parleys in Guwahati and Curachandpur. I still have a bullet in my drawer, which I earned at Churachandpur. Peace came at last in 1998.

In the Bodo-Adivasi conflict around Kokrajhar, Assam during 1996-97 a similar number of people died and over 200,000 were rendered homeless. At least 180,000 people still remain in refugee camps. The Church earned credibility among the people doing relief work for several months, with the bishops themselves directly involved in relief operations and peace efforts. They organized a series of peace-meetings at Guwahati, Kokrajhar and Gossaigaon until the hostilities ceased. About five percent of the two communities may be Catholic; most are non-Christians.

There has been interpositioning between the Kukis and the Paites and the situation has stabilized. Peace has also come between the Bodos and the Adivas, but some issues remain unresolved.

It was my good fortune to have been able, with the help of my ecumenical friends, not only to organize activities (including peace meetings, campaigns, rallies, prayer-gatherings, symbolic actions, signature campaigns, and peace clubs) and to produce educational material like booklets, posters and slogans, but also to have been closely associated with direct peace negotiations. The following are a few of my learnings from my peacemaking experience.

With increasing instances of violence the world over, peacemaking has become a central and urgent task of every citizen. We have been fed for over a century on philosophies of struggle, and have been inspired by the ideals for fighting for justice and battling for our rights. Our combative spirit has grown, while our reconciling skills have sagged.

If, in a conflict, we take for granted that one side is definitely right and another side assuredly wrong, that one is a demon and another a helpless victim, that we have to take sides and fight to the finish, we shall not succeed in becoming mediators between the two.

Most contenders in the fray are convinced that they are fighting for a good cause. They claim that they are wrestling for justice for their own people. Correspondingly, we will find that the other side too is waging a war on behalf of fairness to their community or set of interests. Thus, perceptions of justice clash. And when justice clashes with justice, the peacemaker becomes helpless. So the first learning from experience in this area of peacemaking is that the peacemaker should be prepared to fail.

The next learning is this: *you will not be in a position to initiate a reconciliation-dialogue with contending groups unless you have a measure of sympathy for their cause in your heart.* Excessive preaching and pacifist platitudes in the early stages of dialogue will sound provocative and humiliating to them. Hasty condemnations will enrage them. Even if you believe that their claims are exaggerated, unless you can empathize with them at a deep level and are touched by the passion they have for their goals and the sense of justice that motivates them or their approach to the problem, or at least some aspect of their cause, they will not open out to you. But if you are profoundly struck by the magnitude of their grievances and are able to understand (not necessarily approve) the excesses to which their legitimate anger (at least the way they think) has driven them, they will gradually, and with caution, begin to respond. The same will be true of the other party as well.

Neither group is asking you to condone their immoderation; they are asking you to understand how they felt compelled to go to such lengths. They are not asking you to say much, but feel much. *They are not asking you to appropriate their anger, but to experience their pain in the inhuman situation in which they are imprisoned at the moment (which, of course, they themselves had a share in creating).*

Winning Credibility

Another learning we gather from peacemaking experience is that *there is a profound longing for peace even in the heart of the sternest combatant.* But peace at what terms? On whose terms? Not certainly at the cost of a party's central interests. Not certainly at the price of having to compromise their honor or damage their image. If the peacemaker wants to retain his or her credibility, it must be clear to the contestants that he or she is not going to sell out the gains they have made during a lengthy struggle or compromise their future; that he or she understands that they were driven to violence only because they wanted to convey a message most powerfully to everyone.

The peacemaker begins by interacting with the two groups that are in hostile relationships. If he or she presents himself or herself as a self-appointed mediator or arbitrator, he or she will be rejected. If the peacemaker has already earned a measure of credibility through the evidence of neutral stands and convincing works, he or she begins with an advantage.

Criticizing one party to the other is not the best way of proving his neutrality. *A commitment to humanity that comes through in one's words, deeds, and relationships is far more convincing.* A universal outlook, a sensitivity to human pain no matter who suffers, a keen desire to come to the assistance of people in anxiety -- these are some of the qualities that a peacemaker needs to have.

Getting the Right People for Dialogue

As battles rage, bringing the right people together from the two communities for negotiations itself is an achievement. Now, who are the right people? It is not likely that the frontline fighters will come to talk. Their skills lie in another direction. It is not likely either that the war hawks will deign to dialogue. They have a vested interest in keeping the fires burning. I would describe the people who matter in a peace-dialogue as "socially important people": people who are respected in society; groups whose opinions have wide acceptability among both radicals and moderates; persons like thinkers, writers, speakers and others who stir society with their charismatic leadership or prophetic utterances.

Do not be bewildered by these qualifications. Very often the "big" person is a small person. He or she may not be a graduate. He or she may even be illiterate. He or she may be a humble, soft-spoken person, a stocky and stunted figure. But he or she is a perceptive person, and has the ear of the militant "boss" and his or her confederates. We know that the doer is not always the thinker. He or she acts fast, but does not always reflect. So, after organizing a few agitations, the doer is exhausted; or after killing a few harmless people and causing severe injury on the other party, he or she runs short of ideas, and the entire movement fizzles out. It is the thinker that interprets history, constructs a theory, visualizes a future in order to sustain the movement. I am not necessarily referring to just one person. There may be many at different levels of the hierarchy scattered in the various units.

A last learning is this: it is not enough to send a routine letter of invitation to the participants in the parleys. The peacemaker may have to do a certain amount of personal canvassing (directly or through respected representatives) to make sure that key people will not be missing or else she or he may be greatly disappointed with the turnout.

Actual Dialogue

There are times when negotiators representing conflicting interests will feel unprepared to meet each other. Even if they are already at the venue, they may feel emotionally and mentally not yet ready for direct discussions. It would be best that they spend some period of time in separate gatherings, to thrash out their own two separate points of view, and get themselves ready for actual negotiations. Some time also may be very profitably spent at a common gathering of all the participants of both the parties, in which the peacemaker or some other neutral animator(s) may make a passionate appeal for peace, basing themselves on arguments from human experience, philosophical thought, wisdom of the respective societies, (and if they are believers) teaching of the scriptures. Depending on the charisma and moral authority of the animator(s) a great measure of mental transformation may take place during such an exercise. Experience is witness to this fact.

It is only when both parties feel ready to meet each other, does the peacemaker invite them to come together. After a few motivating words from the peace-team, one spokesperson from each side places the entire problem before the general assembly as his/her group perceives it, expresses his/her desire for peace, points to possible difficulties, proposes solutions and alternatives, invokes collaboration from the other side in the most acceptable way possible, and concludes. After this there may be common discussions to deepen the understanding of the problem and of each others' position on the entire matter. A few rounds of separate and common meetings to narrow the differences and widen the areas of consensus may bring the participants to the final stage and conclusions. Often such meetings fail and the peacemaker has to be begin all over again.

I would suggest that during the entire period of the negotiations the peacemaker remains merely helpful and intelligent, leaving full freedom to the contestants to thrash out their differences. Only during a deadlock should he or she offer some suggestions, mostly regarding procedures. Occasionally it may serve to draw the attention of the debaters to some point of view they had overlooked. The less he or

107

she presses his or her vision, his or her course of action or set of solutions on the participants the better. If the solutions are the contestants' own, they have a better chance of winning wide acceptance and of being implemented.

The best role of the peacemaker is that of a confidence-builder, facilitator, creator of a serene atmosphere...an atmosphere in which interactions become easy. If he or she remains inconspicuous and keeps a low-profile, the long-term contribution can be greater. But the temptation to win recognition and wide acclaim is so great, that the peacemaker, if successful, rushes into the roles of a mediator, arbitrator and judge. Even if the contestants agree to such an idea, it would be unwise to assume such roles. Winning the headlines may be flattering, but the fruits therefrom may not last long. The simple reason is that the solutions you propose are not theirs. *Doing things as though not doing it –that is the role of the true peacemaker.*

Premature publicity is fatal to the cause. By this I do not mean to say she should keep media at a distance. But he or she should feel free from having to play up to the gallery. He or she should not give chance to those opposing the cause of peace to track him down at every step and make him stumble. If he or she is not careful they can undermine his initiatives long before they begin to yield fruits. That is why I say premature publicity can leave you exposed.

Living together always means being prepared for compromises. This is true of a family, a village, a nation or the international community. The most valuable contribution the peacemaking team can make is to lead opposing partners towards a gradual awareness of this great truth. Self evident as it is, if you rush to conclusions urging compromise and quoting adages and aphorisms when the anger is still high, the pedagogic process you have initiated may be disturbed. It is far more profitable to draw their attention to the disastrous consequences of ongoing conflict. You have to walk a long distance with them sharing the pain of their people. Only when they are mentally prepared to look for alternative solutions, is it pedagogical to propose compromises.

It is unwise too to prompt specific issues on which a compromise may be worked out. It is best that they emerge from the participants' lived experience and their own agonizing search for a way out of the deadlock they are caught up in. Prodding compromises in the area of their central concerns may appear insensitive to them. What they themselves are ultimately willing to concede is their gift to God in view of the future of their community and that of humanity.

Often the negotiators have no authority to decide on issues on behalf of the two contending parties. But they can make recommendations. And if these are well-phrased, balanced and responsive to realities, they may evoke a good reaction. The participants in the first trend-setting meeting we have described above, can make an effort to organize similar meetings at the local level, try to reproduce the same atmosphere and goodwill, and discuss the recommendations that they have drawn up for the public. Each party will do this with their own people and then with others. If there is wide acceptance of the proposals, the communities may move on to final negotiations in the presence of civil authorities, in which the peacemaker need not take part at all. If in the process he or she is forgotten or is marginalized, he or she should rejoice, for it is God who is the author of peace no matter who serves the cause.

Problems Related to Peacemaking

The problems that the peacemaker will have to face are of infinite variety. There may be stiff opposition to the entire effort from interested parties on either side. The peacemaker may appear a threat to militants committed to violence and to those benefiting from the insecurity created by armed conflict. *If you wish to be a peacemaker and save the lives of others, be prepared for death.* Several peacemakers have given their lives for their cause in recent history, Mahatma Gandhi and Martin Luther King, Jr.

Negotiators whom the peacemaker contacted may refuse to put in an appearance. Their ears may be poisoned against Christian initiatives. Follow-up efforts may never take off. People may get discouraged due to the recurrence of violence. Collective anger may be rekindled if their community is hit again unexpectedly. Malicious rumors may be deliberately spread. The press may inflate the number of victims attributing wrong motives, interpret the issues wrongly, ignore peace-initiatives and successes or allege negative intentions.

The peacemaker may come across another type of difficulty as the dialogue progresses. It will appear as though words have changed their meanings. For example, someone may be using the word 'justice' to refer to the advantage of one's own community only, not of others. By 'peace' one may mean retaining in serenity a whole lot of ill-gotten goods. 'Democracy' may mean doing as one pleases, freedom to do injustice, or total chaos. Sometimes discussions cannot make headway because the contestants have their own style of using words, their own way of interpreting history, their own strategies of making allegations, their own fashion of creating myths. The peacemaker should not give up.

If memories of historic injuries are alive in people's hearts and if negative stereotypes of each other have developed, it will be difficult to solve the problem in a short time. In such a case, every peace agreement is a truce. Hostilities may be renewed any time. But the peacemaker finds renewed strength and motivation in her faith and love. He or she is ready to begin all over again and gets busy with the healing of historic injuries and demolishing of stereotypes. And God will be with the peacemaker.

Peace is God's Gift

Nothing is lost in God. Peace comes in God's own good time, independently of all that the peacemaker can do. The fighting may end for many reasons: weapons run short; fighters are exhausted; government and army pressure mounts; good sense comes to prevail. But work continues for the peacemaker, whose human effort remains on like the flickering lamp over the high altar, which speaks of a Presence and whispers hope.

There are many ways in which God makes people beat swords into ploughshares. But when God's peace comes at last, there is sunshine and joy over every hill and in every valley. It is a sunshine that pierces the secret thoughts of every heart, dispelling gloom and holding out hopes.

Franciscan Publications for Transformative Nonviolence

The Justice, Peace, and Integrity of Creation Resource Book

Available in English, German, French, Italian and Spanish at: http://www.ofm-jpic.org/handbook/index.html

(The book is in Adobe format, and you will need to download the free Acrobat Reader from Adobe in order to read the manual from the web site.)

In 1999 the Office of Justice, Peace and Integrity of Creation (JPIC) of the Order of Friars Minor made available a resource book to help Franciscans become more conscious of the fact that the Franciscan commitment to justice, peace and the integrity of creation is an integral part of Franciscan Spirituality. The book has articles on Franciscan Spirituality, on the Franciscan option for the poor, on encouragement for prayer and meditation, on incarnated action in concrete situations in the light of Justice, Peace and Integrity of Creation.

Instruments of Peace - Led by the Spirit

Available in English and Spanish at:
http://www.ofm-jpic.org/congress2000/index.html

This book, a supplement to the JPIC Manual, contains a series of presentations made at the first International Congress for all OFM JPIC provincial animators in Vossenack, Germany, in October 2000. It continues to make the point that JPIC is an integral part of the Franciscan charism. The challenge for all Franciscans is to integrate JPIC into their personal and fraternal lives as well as into their ministries.

From Violence to Wholeness:
A Ten-Part Process in the Spirituality and
Practice of Active Nonviolence

From Violence To Wholeness is a nonviolence education program from Pace e Bene Nonviolence Service. It assists people from all walks of life to recognize and make contact with the power of transformative nonviolence; to deepen the spiritual grounding of nonviolence; to acquire and sharpen skills for putting this into practice; to become deeply grounded agents of nonviolent transformation of violent and unjust social structures; and to become artisans of a more just and compassionate world. This 179-page book is comprised of agendas and readings for 10 two-hour sessions exploring the spirituality and practice of active nonviolence for personal and social transformation. Available in *English, Spanish,* and *French.* The cost: $19.95 USD per book ($15.95 for 5 or more), plus $4.00 (for the first copy) and $1.00 (for each additional copy) for shipping and handling.

To order, please contact:
Pace e Bene Nonviolence Service
1420 W. Bartlett Ave., Las Vegas, NV 89106 USA
Tel: 702-648-2281
E-mail: fvtw@paceebene.org
Website: www.paceebene.org

Working for Reconciliation: A Caritas Handbook

E-mail: caritas.internationalis@caritas.va

Published in 1999 and 2001, this book is available in English, French and Spanish from Caritas Internationalis, Piazzo San Calisto 16, Vatican City. A new book was expected to be published in September 2002 entitled *"Peace Building: A Caritas Training Manual"* available in English, French and Spanish.

A Select List of Nonviolence Organizations and Internet Resources on Nonviolence

Franciscans International
Geneva office: P.O. Box 104 CH-1211, Geneva 20 - Switzerland
Tel.: 41 (22) 919-4010
E-mail: geneve@fiop.org

New York office: 211 East 43rd Street, Room 1100, New York, NY 10017-4707
Tel: 212-490-4624
Fax: 212-283-0134
E-mail: franintl@franciscansinternational.org
Website: www.FranciscansInternational.org

North America website: www.fi-na.org (many links to peace and Franciscan sites).

Pace e Bene Nonviolence Service
1420 W. Bartlett Ave., Las Vegas, NV 89106 USA
Tel.: 702-648-2281

E-mail: peterediger@paceebene.org
Website: www.paceebene.org
Projects: **From Violence To Wholeness**, **Paz y Bien, and Nurturing a Culture of Nonviolence**

Capacitar

23 East Beach Street, Suite 206
Watsonville, CA 95076 USA
Tel: 831-722-7590
Fax: 831-722-7703
E-mail: capacitar@capacitar.org
Website: www.capacitar.org
An international network for healing and personal and social transformation of the effects of trauma and conflict

Christian Peacemaker Teams

P.O. Box 6508
Chicago, IL 60680 USA
Tel: 773-277-0253
Fax: 773-277-0291
E-mail: cpt@igc.org
Website: www.prairienet.org/cpt/

Fellowship of Reconciliation

P.O. Box 271

Nyack, NY 10960 USA
Tel: 845-358-4601
Fax: 845-358-4924
E-mail: for@forusa.org
Website: www.forusa.org

M.K. Gandhi Institute for Nonviolence
C/o Christian Brothers University
650 East Parkway, South
Memphis, TN 38104 USA
Tel: 901-452-2824
Fax: 901-452-2775
E-mail: questions@gandhiinstitute.org
Website: www.gandhiinstitute.org

Nonviolence International
4545 42nd Street, NW Suite 209
Washington D.C. 20016 USA
Tel: 202-244-0951
Email: info@nonviolenceinternational.net

The Nonviolence Web
P.O. Box 38504
Philadelphia, PA 19104 USA
Tel: 215-681-0783
E-mail: nvweb@nonviolence.org

Website: www.nonviolence.org
Includes an e-magazine and many links to key
nonviolence organizations throughout the world.

Pax Christi International
Rue du Vieux Marche aux Grains 21
1000 Brussels, Belgium.
Tel.: 32/2/502.55.50
Fax: 32/2/502.46.26
E-mail: hello@paxchristi.net
Website: www.paxchristi.net

**Servicio Paz y Justicia en America Latina
(SERPAJ)**
J. Requena 1642
11200 Montevideo - Uruguay
Tel: (598 2) 408 32 45
Fax: (598 2) 408 32 45
E-mail: serpajal@internet.com.uy
Website: www.nonviolence.org/serpaj

Select Bibliography on Nonviolence

- Peter Ackerman and Jack Duvall, *A Force More Powerful: A Century of Nonviolent Conflict* (New York: St. Martin's Press, 2000).

- Elise Boulding, *Cultures of Peace and the Hidden Side of History* (Syracuse, NY: Syracuse University Press, 2000).

- Ken Butigan with Patricia Bruno, O.P., *From Violence To Wholeness: The Spirituality and Practice of Active Nonviolence* (Berkeley, CA: Pace e Bene, 2002).

- Patricia Cane, Ph.D., *Trauma Healing and Transformation: Awakening a New Heart with Body Mind Spirit Practices* (Watsonville, CA: Capacitar, 2000). Contact: 23 East Beach, Suite 206, Watsonville, CA 95076.

- Richard Deats, "The Global Spread of Nonviolence," *Fellowship* (July/August 1996). Reprints available from FOR, Box 271, Nyack, NY 10960. 1 copy: $1.00.

- Leonard Desroches, *Allow the Water: Anger, Fear, Power, Work, Sexuality, and the Spirituality and Practice of Active Nonviolence* (Toronto, Ontario: Dunamis Publishers). Contact: 407 Bleeker St., Toronto, Ontario, Canada M4X 1W2.

- Eileen Egan, *Peace Be With You: Justified Warfare or the Way of Nonviolence* (Maryknoll, NY: Orbis Books, 1999).

- Bernie Glassman, *Bearing Witness* (New York: Bell Tower, 1998).

119

- Michael Henderson, *Forgiveness: Breaking the Chain of Hate* (Wilsonville, OR: Book Partners, 1999).

- Robert H. King, *Thomas Merton and Thich Nhat Hanh: Engaged Spirituality in an Age of Globalization* (New York and London: Continuum, 2001).

- Pam McAlister, *You Can't Kill the Spirit: Stories of Women and Nonviolent Action* (Philadelphia: New Society Publishers, 1988).

- Philip McManus and Gerald Schlabach, eds., *Relentless Persistence: Nonviolent Action in Latin America* (Philadelphia: New Society Publishers, 1991).

- Bill Moyer, *Doing Democracy: The MAP Model for Organizing Social Movements* (Gabriola Island, BC: New Society Publishers, 2001).

- Michael Nagler, *Is There No Other Way? The Search for a Nonviolent Future* (Berkeley, CA: Berkeley Hills Books, 2001).

- Roger S. Powers and William B. Vogele, eds., *Protest, Power, and Change: An Encyclopedia of Nonviolent Action* (New York: Garland Publishing, 1997).

- Alain Richard, "Concerning Nonviolence and the Franciscan Movement," *The Cord*, May 1989, republished in the Pace e Bene Occasional Paper Series No.1.

- Elisabeth Schüssler Fiorenza and Shawn Copeland, editors, *Violence Against Women* (Maryknoll, NY: Orbis Books, 1994).

- Walter Wink, *Engaging the Powers: Discernment and Resistance in a World of Domination* (Minneapolis: Fortress, 1992).

- Walter Wink, ed., Peace is the Way: Writings on Nonviolence from the Fellowship of Reconciliation (Maryknoll, NY: Orbis, 2000).

End Notes

1. St. Bonaventure, *The Journey of the Mind to God,* translated by Philotheus Boehner, O.F.M., edited with introduction by Stephen F. Brown (Indianapolis/ Cambridge: Hackett Publishing Company, 1993), p. 1.

2. Regis J. Armstrong, O.F.M. Cap., Wayne Hellman, O.F.M. Conv., and William Short, O.F.M., eds., *Francis of Assisi: Early Documents, Vol. I, The Saint* (Hyde Park, NY: New City Press, 1999), p. 136.

3. Marie Dennis, Cynthia Moe-Lobeda, Joseph Nangle, O.F.M., and Stuart Taylor, *St. Francis and the Foolishness of God* (Maryknoll, NY: Orbis Books, 1999), p. 86.

4. Alain Richard, O.F.M., "Concerning Nonviolence and the Franciscan Movement," *The Cord*, May 1989, republished in the Pace e Bene Occasional Paper Series No.1, p. l.

5. Walter Wink, *Engaging the Powers: Discernment and Resistance in a World of Domination* (Minneapolis: Fortress Press, 1992), p. 100.

6. Wink, P. 101-111.

7. Regis J. Armstrong, O.F.M. Cap., Wayne Hellman, O.F.M. Conv., and William Short, O.F.M., eds., *Francis of Assisi: Early Documents, Vol. II, The Founder* (Hyde Park, NY: New City Press, 2000)., p. 69. Verse 4 of the Legend of the Three Companions.

8. Regis J. Armstrong, O.F.M. Cap., Wayne Hellman, O.F.M. Conv., and William Short, O.F.M., eds., *Francis of Assisi: Early Documents, Vol. II, The Founder* (Hyde Park, NY: New City Press, 2000)., p. 71. Verse 6 of the Legend of the Three Companions.

9. Arnaldo Fortini, *Francis of Assisi* translated by Helen Moak (New York: Crossroad, 1981) p. 140.

10. Fortini, pp. 154-155.

11. Regis J. Armstrong, O.F.M. Cap., Wayne Hellman, O.F.M. Conv., and William Short, O.F.M., eds., *Francis of Assisi: Early Documents, Vol. I, The Saint* (Hyde Park, NY: New City Press, 1999), p. 184. 1 Celano, verse 4.

12. Herman Schaluck, O.F.M., *The Anthonian*, St. Anthony's Guild: New York, 1995, pp. 22-23.

13. Regis J. Armstrong, O.F.M. Cap., Wayne Hellman, O.F.M. Conv., and William Short, O.F.M., eds., *Francis of Assisi: Early Documents, Vol. I, The Saint* (Hyde Park, NY: New City Press, 1999), p. 48.

14. Regis J. Armstrong, O.F.M. Cap., Wayne Hellman, O.F.M. Conv., and William Short, O.F.M., eds., *Francis of Assisi: Early Documents, Vol. I, The Saint* (Hyde Park, NY: New City Press, 1999), p. 126, verse 23.

15. Bonaventure, *The Journey of the Mind to God*, translated by Philotheus Boehner, O.F.M., edited with introduction by Stephen F. Brown (Indianapolis/Cambridge: Hackett Publishing Company, 1993), p. 1.

16. This story is told in Michael Henderson's book, *Forgiveness: Breaking the Chain of Hate (Wilsonville, OR: Book Partners, 1999)* pp. 133-137.

17. Regis J. Armstrong, O.F.M. Cap., and Ignatius C. Brady, O.F.M. with a preface by John Vaughn, O.F.M. *Francis and Clare: The Complete Works* (New York: Paulist Press, 1982), p. 211. Chapter II, verse 1 from the Rule of Saint Clare.

18. Armstrong and Brady, Francis and Clare: The Complete Works, p. 215. The Rule of Saint Clare, Chapter IV, verse 1.

19. Ibid., Chapter IV, verse 5.

20. Ibid., p. 216. Chapter IV, verse 10.

21. Ibid., Chapter IV, verse 11.

22. Ibid., Chapter IV, verse 13.

23. Ibid., Chapter IV, verse 16.

24. Regis J. Armstrong, O.F.M. Cap., and Ignatius C. Brady, O.F.M. with a preface by John Vaughn, O.F.M. *Francis and Clare: The Complete Works* (New York: Paulist Press, 1982), pp. 199-202. vv.4 and 42, 3rd letter to Agnes.

25. Gwenole Jeusset, O.F.M., "The Incarnation in Relation to Other Religions, specifically Islam," address to the General Assembly of the International Conference of Third Order Regular Franciscans, Assisi, May, 2001.

26. Regis J. Armstrong, O.F.M. Cap., Wayne Hellman, O.F.M. Conv., and William Short, O.F.M., eds., *Francis of Assisi: Early Documents, Vol. III, The Prophet* (Hyde Park, NY: New City Press, 2001), pp. 601-3.

27. Regis J. Armstrong, O.F.M. Cap., Wayne Hellman, O.F.M. Conv., and William Short, O.F.M., eds., *Francis of Assisi: Early Documents, Vol. I, The Saint* (Hyde Park, NY: New City Press, 1999), p. 581. The story of a pilgrimage to the Holy Lands is mentioned in most of the accounts of Francis's life. However, the earliest reference to this pilgrimage is found only in 1321 in the writings of Angelo Clareno. As Friar Gwenole Jeusset O.F.M. points out, the accounts of this event in Francis's life were heavily influenced by the anti-Muslim stance of thirteenth century hagiographers. For this reason, rather than presenting this story from any of those early accounts of Francis, we have quoted from the contemporary version by Jacques de Vitry.

28. Gwenole Jeusset, O.F.M., "The Incarnation in Relation to Other Religions, specifically Islam," address to the General Assembly of the International Conference of Third Order Regular Franciscans held in Assisi, May 2001.

29. Chapter 16 of Francis's Early Rule.

30. Michael Hadley, *The Justice Tree: Multifaith Reflection on Criminal Justice* (Albany NY: State University of New York Press, 2001). This book is a synopsis of "The Spiritual Roots of Restorative Justice Project," of the

Center for Studies in Religion and Society, University of Victoria, Victoria, British Columbia, Canada.

31. Regis J. Armstrong, O.F.M. Cap., Wayne Hellman, O.F.M. Conv., and William Short, O.F.M., eds., *Francis of Assisi: Early Documents, Vol. III, The Prophet* (Hyde Park, NY: New City Press, 2001), pp. 609-14.

32. Michael Hadley, *The Justice Tree: Multifaith Reflection on Criminal Justice* (Albany NY: State University of New York Press, 2001).

33. Ibid.

34. Regis J. Armstrong, O.F.M. Cap., Clare of Assisi: Early Documents (New York: Paulist Press, 1988), pp. 226-7.

35. The Suore Francescane Insegnanti General Chapter Address, Rome, October, 1999.

36. Michael Henderson, *Forgiveness: Breaking the Chain of Hate* (Wilsonville, OR: Book Partners, 1999), pp. 145-150.

37. Regis J. Armstrong, O.F.M. Cap., Wayne Hellman, O.F.M. Conv., and William Short, O.F.M., eds., *Francis of Assisi: Early Documents, Vol. II, The Founder* (Hyde Park, NY: New City Press, 2000), pp. 187-8.

38. Arnaldo Fortini, *Francis of Assisi* translated by Helen Moak (New York: Crossroad, 1981) p. 569.

39. Fortini, p. 574.

40. Ibid., p. 575.

41. Ibid., p. 576.

42. Walter Wink, *Engaging the Powers*, p. 6.

43. Ibid., p. 9.

44. Ibid., p. 110.

45. Fortini, p. 580.

46. Ibid.

47. Jim Forest, *The Ladder of the Beatitudes,* (Maryknoll, NY: Orbis Books, 1999), p. 125.